Study Starters
Basic Strategies for Academic Success

by
Diane P. Kostick

illustrated by Susan Kropa

Cover by Susan Kropa

Copyright © 1994, Good Apple

ISBN No. 0-86653-797-X

Printing No. 98765

**Good Apple
A Division of Frank Schaffer Publications, Inc.
23740 Hawthorne Boulevard
Torrance, CA 90505-5927**

The purchase of this book entitles the buyer to reproduce the student activity pages for classroom use only. Any other use requires written permission from Good Apple.

All rights reserved. Printed in the United States of America.

Welcome

Students
Teachers
Parents

This book is dedicated to helping you.

Dedication

To Andy, Jolie, Yuri, April, and Mary. Thanks for your time, talent, and technological "know how."

Table of Contents

Introduction vi
Getting It Together 1
   Study Skills 2
   Now It's Your Turn 4
   Learning Ways–Graphic Organizers 5
   SQ3R 6
   KWL (Know, Want to Know, Learned) 7
   Circling and Detailing 8
   Mapping–Alike and Different 9
   Diagramming an Idea 9
   Identifying Problems and Solutions 10
   Now It's Your Turn 11
   How to Outline 15
   Now It's Your Turn 16
   Sentence Diagramming Guide 17
   Your Diagramming Guide 20
   Eight Parts of Speech 21
   Now It's Your Turn 22
   Venn Diagrams 26
   Now It's Your Turn 27
Writing, Writing, Writing 28
   The Web of Writing 29
   The Writing Process 30
   Now It's Your Turn 32
   Narrative Writing–The Art of Storytelling 38
   Irresistible Beginnings and Endings 41
   Now It's Your Turn 44
   Descriptive Writing 50
   Descriptive Writing "Lingo" 53
   Now It's Your Turn 55
   Expository Writing 59
   Now It's Your Turn 62
   Persuasive Writing 66
   Now It's Your Turn 69
   Journals and Diaries 72
   Journal Writing 74
   Now It's Your Turn 75
   Writing Letters and Thank-You Notes 77
   Now It's Your Turn 79
   How to Address an Envelope 81
   Now It's Your Turn 82
   How to Fold a Letter 83
   Getting Published 84
   Now It's Your Turn 90

Make, Take, Invigorate 91
   Book Reports–Forty-Five Ways to Give 'em 92
   Now It's Your Turn 97
   Beautiful Banners 98
   Now It's Your Turn 100
   Creating Collages 102
   Now It's Your Turn 103
   How to Make a Poster 104
   Now It's Your Turn 107
   Making Mobiles 108
   Now It's Your Turn 112
   Puppet People 114
   Now It's Your Turn 115
   Shoe Box Float Projects 116
   Now It's Your Turn 117
Poetry Gives Voice to Our Silent Songs. 118
   The Language of Poets and Poetry 119
   Now It's Your Turn 125
   Haiku, Cinquain, Acrostic, Free Verse, and Limerick 126
   Now It's Your Turn 133
   Who Am I? Poems 137
   Now It's Your Turn 140
   Concrete Poetry 141
   Now It's Your Turn 143
   Diamante 144
   Now It's Your Turn 145
   Index 146
   Bibliography 152

Introduction

Study Starters is designed to give right or left brain oriented students essential tools they need to be successful with school assignments. The book begins by showing students how to get organized, how to make an after-school schedule, and what supplies they need to get them on the right road to academic success.

The Graphic Organizer pages are chock-full of pictorial formulas to teach students how to graph, map, diagram, outline, identify, and arrange information on any topic, for any school subject. Concisely written explanations and provocative visual examples show students how to master many commonly required homework tasks.

Writing, Writing, and More Writing introduces students to four basic writing structures–descriptive, narrative, explanatory, and persuasive. Students are provided with techniques to create vivid images, to apply specific words, and fashion powerful phrases to be utilized in their writing assignments. Professional and student models coach students through the art of writing, and in addition students are provided with a set of blueprints so they can develop and nurture their personal writing needs.

Make, Take, Invigorate demonstrates for students a myriad of methods for how they can create colorful visuals for classroom use to enhance oral reports, book presentations, or class projects. The activities are peppered with specific "how to's" which students can easily emulate.

Poems, Poets, and Poetry examines the wonderful world of literary songsters. Basic poetic terms are defined, student samples are provided, and practical suggestions are offered for students to learn how to write poetry free of fear and stress.

Study Starters was prepared to help teachers who are too busy to teach, to support parents who are too preoccupied to help, and to assist students who are too overburdened to remember all that the teacher wants them to do when assigning homework.

Getting It Together

Study Skills–How Can I Help Myself Cope with School Stuff?

In order to be successful at anything–sports, music, writing, or whatever–you need to frequently practice the skill in order to perfect it. Learning to study requires practice too. Some people study best when the environment is dead quiet, while others prefer to listen to music while they study. Some people study best at the library surrounded by books, encyclopedias, and friends. Other people study best at home, at their desks, surrounded by their own familiar tools, equipment, and supplies. You need to determine in which environment you work best because all students need to study and all students need to develop good study skills.

What Equipment Do I Need?*

- Desk or writing surface with the right amount of light

- Paper, pencils, pens, erasers, colored pencils, markers

- Ruler, compass, protractor, stapler

- Dictionary, thesaurus, atlas, encyclopedia, almanac

- Newspaper, magazines

* You don't need all the equipment listed to be a good student, but the more items you have on the list, the easier it will be for you to get down to the business of studying.

Studying requires a lot of concentration, a lot of determination, a lot of self-discipline. One of the best ways to learn how to study is to establish a study-habit schedule. To help you do this, examine the following chart. It is a study schedule that was created by Craig Sohl, a junior high school student. Note that Craig put in place those times he knew he was busy with an after school sports activity, and he also filled in the time he knew his family has dinner. In addition, being realistic and being someone who likes to watch TV, Craig "plugged in" time to watch his favorite programs too. Note, however, that he also included Sunday in his schedule because he knows that he must get himself ready on Sunday nights for the coming school week. If Craig does not have homework in the subject areas listed on a particular night, he uses that time to study his class notes or to go over pages in his textbook for the class. Craig understands that to develop a study habit, one must set aside time to study, not merely fill the time with homework tasks.

Craig Sohl's Study Schedule

	Mon.	Tues.	Wed.	Thurs.	Fri.	Sun.
3:30	Wrestling	Wrestling	Wrestling	Wrestling	Wrestling	Free Time
4:00	Snack & TV	Snack & TV	Snack & TV	Snack & TV	Snack & TV	Free Time
4:30	English	English	English	English	English	English
5:00	Math	Math	Math	Math	Math	Math
5:30	Science	Science	Science	Science	Science	Science
6:00	Dinner	Dinner	Dinner	Dinner	Dinner	Dinner
6:30	Dinner	Dinner	Dinner	Dinner	Dinner	Dinner
7:00	TV	TV	TV	TV	TV	TV
7:30	TV	TV	TV	TV	TV	TV
8:00	Social Studies	Social Studies	Social Studies	Social Studies	Social Studies	Social Studies
8:30	Snack & Read	Snack & Read	Snack & Read	Snack & Read	Snack & Read	Snack & Read
9:00	Bedtime	Bedtime	Bedtime	Bedtime	Bedtime	Bedtime

Now It's Your Turn
My Study Schedule

	Mon.	Tues.	Wed.	Thur.	Fri.	Sun.
3:00						
3:30						
4:00						
4:30						
5:00						
5:30						
6:00						
6:30						
7:00						
7:30						
8:00						
8:30						
9:00						
9:30						

Learning Ways– Graphic Organizers

SQ3R

Every student has his or her own approach and techniques for learning. That is to be expected, as people have their own unique rules for effective learning; but there are general rules for learning that can be utilized by all kinds of learners. What are the rules?

One effective rule was developed and soundly tested at Ohio State University. It is a five-step technique called *SQ3R*. The first step in the process, *survey*, means to skim the material for the best possible overall picture of what you are going to study before you study it in detail. For example, in a chapter of a book, look over the headings, figure out the main idea of each paragraph, and pay attention to any boldface or italicized words. You know that they will be important. In addition, if the book has any tables, graphs, charts, maps, or illustrations, examine them to get a better overview of the information you will be learning in the text.

The second step, *Q*, stands for *question*. Questions help you learn because they make you think about what you want and might need to know before you read or study. Prereading questions enables you to focus on answers you will seek in your reading. The 5 W's are good question-asking starting points. The 5 W's are who, what, where, when, why, and sometimes how. You should make a mental or physical list of questions you have about the material you are going to study before you begin an in-depth study of it.

Read, *recite*, and *review* make up the third step in the process. At this stage, you are ready to carefully and actively read the material, to recite and recall for yourself what you have read, and to reread, if necessary, to be sure that you thoroughly understand and can summarize the information you have studied.

Keep in mind that the system works only if you apply yourself to the task at hand. Practice makes the *SQ3R* method become automatic. Remember, too, that you will use the *SQ3R* method differently for science than you will for math. Students who have learned this method have been able to improve their grades, sometimes enormously.

Animals, Animals, Animals

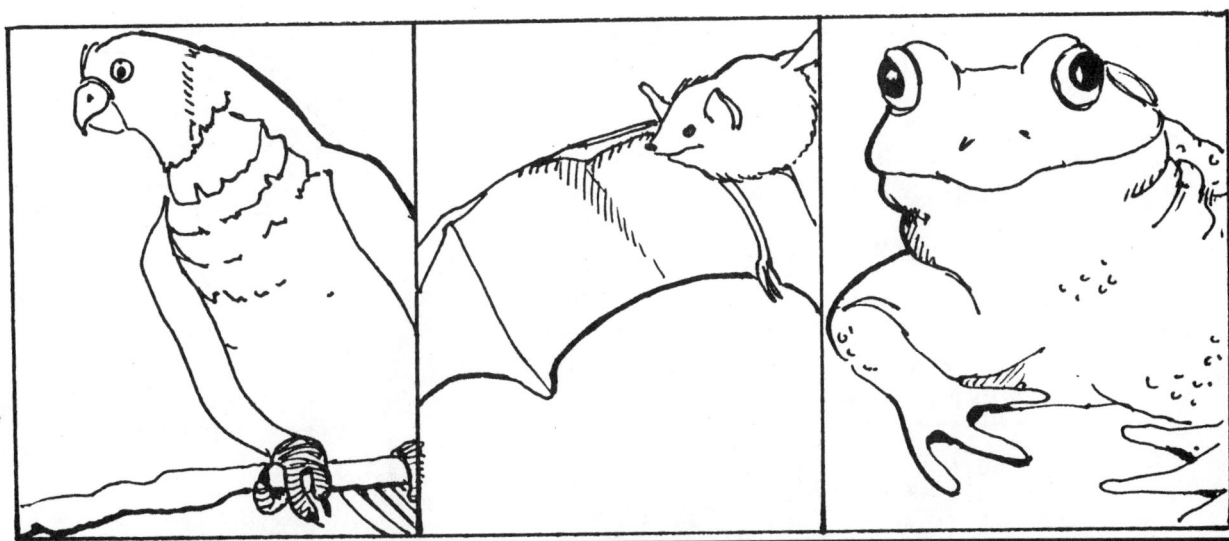

Know	Want to Know	Learned
• Animals have local motion, that is they readily move from place to place. • A parrot eats nuts and seeds. It squawks with its noisy, noisy voice.	• How do snakes move about without legs? • What guides do animals use to migrate from place to place? • How do bats fly?	• Birds and insects are mammals. • A frog can jump, swim, and croak because its body is "programmed to." • There are six animal classes: mammals, birds, fish, anthropods, reptiles, and amphibians.

Another technique to help you recall what you have studied is referred to as the *KWL* technique. The letters stand for the following: list what you *Know*, list what you *Want* to know, and list what you have *Learned*. This will help you pick out the main ideas, recall important terms, and organize the materials you have read or studied so that you will remember them in a graphic, vivid way.

There are at least six ways to create "picture maps" to help you retain what you have learned. They are circling and detailing a topic, mapping for comparison and contrast, diagramming main ideas, graphing cause and effect, identifying problems and solutions, and outlining logical sequences. The techniques are suitable to a variety of subjects from history to science, from English to French, from math to music, and from grammar to geography.

Here is how the system works. The first is called circling. You put the main idea in the center of the circle and radiate the details of the topic around the circle. The next couple of pages show you how to use the rest of these techniques. One special learning tool is called a Venn diagram; two pages are devoted to it.

Circling and Detailing

Milky Way | Solar System | Copernicus

Graphing

Cause	Effect
• My jogging shoes are worn out.	• I can't jog in the marathon.
• I spent all my money on clothes.	• I can't go to the show tonight.
• The muddy dog jumped on my new suit.	• My suit will need to be cleaned.
• "The temperatures will soar to 85 degrees today," predicted the meteorologist.	• The children wore shorts and short-sleeved shirts to school.
• My dad's car ran out of gas.	• My dad had to walk to the gas station.
• The toaster didn't work right.	• The raisin bread got burnt to a crisp.

Mapping:

| Abraham Lincoln | Alike (Compare) | Frederick A. Douglass |

- Born in 1800s
- Came from poor families
- Self-educated
- Great orators
- Changed public opinion regarding the rights of Black Americans
- Left a mark on history

Different (Contrast)

- Born free
- Most effective as a public speaker
- Worked for freedom of slaves through governmental processes
- Rejected violence as a means of freeing the slaves
- Died in 1865

- Born a slave
- Most effective as a journalist
- Ran a branch of the Underground Railroad
- Accepted the necessity of violence in order to free slaves
- Died in 1895

Diagramming an Idea:

Jazz — Kinds of Music — Classical
Rap — Kinds of Music — Secular
Rock 'n' Roll — Kinds of Music — Religious

Identifying:

The Twentieth Century

Problems ⟶ **Solutions**

Problems	Solutions
• Lack of mass transportation	• Study mass transportation in other countries to find ways to improve ours
• Health care for all	• Investigate a variety of ways to provide health care for all citizens
• Pollution	• Explore systems to clean the air and water worldwide
• Gangs	• Set up task force of police, social workers, educators, parents to combat gangs
• AIDS	• Provide funding for education and research to eliminate the disease
• Unemployment	• Give tax incentives to businesses to expand their operations
• Endangered species	• Create a worldwide scientific team to provide protection for endangered flora and fauna
• School dropouts	• Create alternative schools for potential dropouts, giving them job training

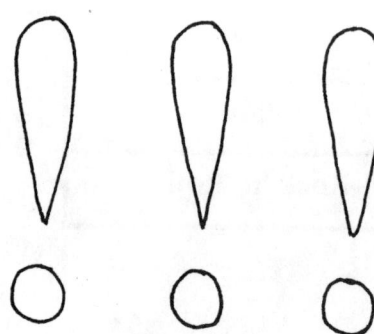

Now It's Your Turn

My topic is _____.

Know	Want to Know	Learned

Now It's Your Turn

Circling and Detailing

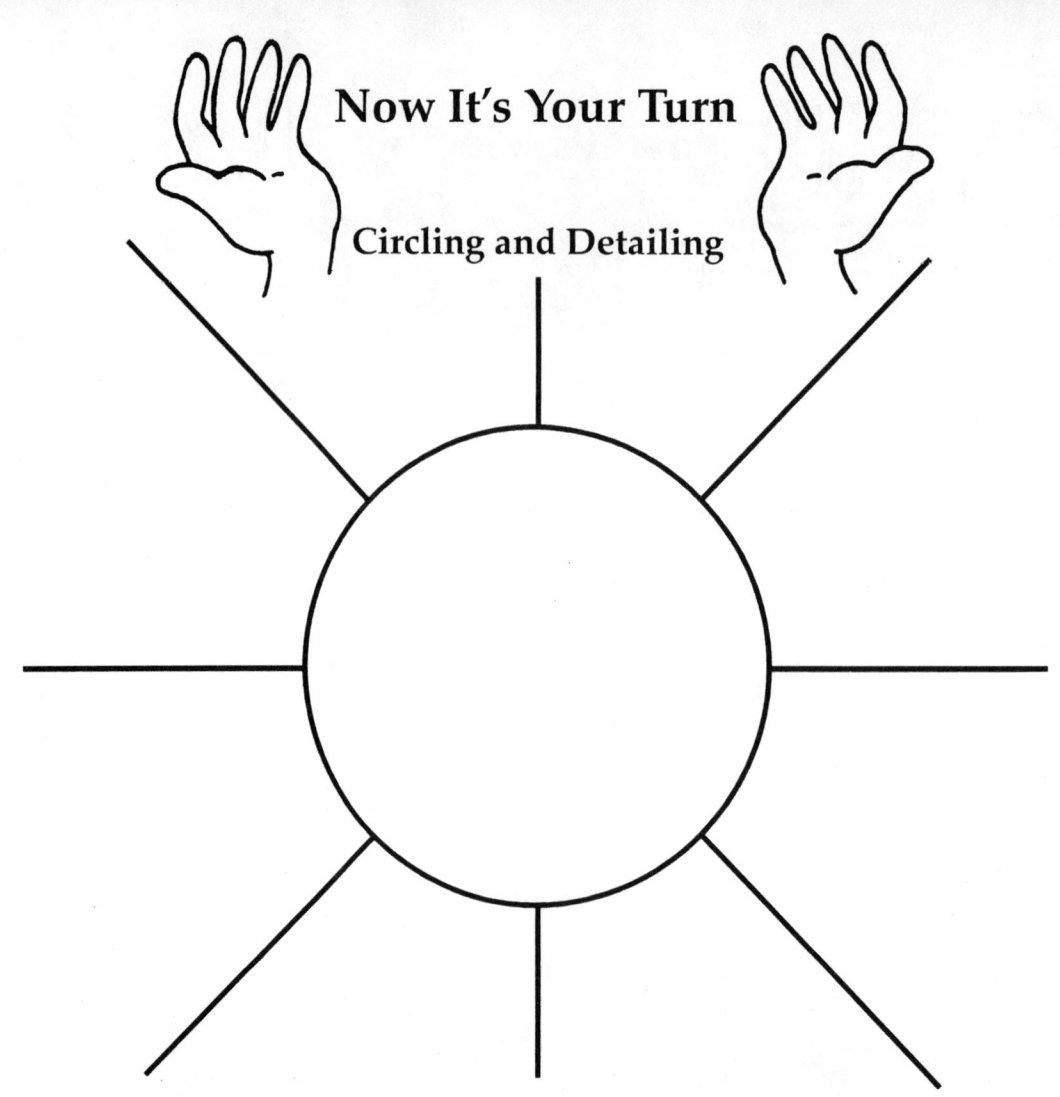

Graphing

Cause	Effect

Mapping

Alike
(Compare)

Different
(Contrast)

Diagramming an Idea

Identifying

Problems → Solutions

How to Outline

An outline is a plan that writers, speakers, and even coaches use before they decide to commit words to paper, words to an audience, or words to a team roster. It is a handy system for organizing your work. Preparing an outline allows you to pick out the most important things in your material and then enables you to put the necessary details in their proper places. There is a definite form for an outline and one that you can easily learn.

The most important ideas in an outline are labeled with Roman numerals beginning with I, II, etc. The less important ideas are labeled with capital letters A, B, etc. Under the capital letters are the Arabic numerals, 1, 2, etc. And beneath the Arabic numerals are the lower case letters of the alphabet, a, b, etc. Notice that outline parts always come in pairs: if there is a "I" there is a "II," if there is an "A" there is a "B" and so on. Here is what an outline looks like.

	Soccer
I. _____	I. History of the game
A. _____	A. 400 B.C.–200s A.D.
B. _____	B. 1800–2000 A.D.
II. _____	II. The field and equipment
III. _____	III. How the game is played
A. _____	A. Players and officials
B. _____	B. Rules
1. _____	1. International
a. _____	a. North American
b. _____	b. European and Latin American
2. _____	2. Professional Leagues

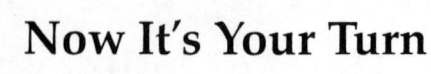

Now It's Your Turn

Now you are ready to make an outline on your own. You can pick any topic you wish. Use the outline on the previous page to guide you in placing the various details of information you want in their proper places.

Topic:_____

I. _____

    A. _____

    B. _____

II. _____

III. _____

    A. _____

    B. _____

        1. _____

            a. _____

            b. _____

        2. _____

            a. _____

            b. _____

Sentence Diagramming Guide

Diagramming sentences is the "arithmetic" of English. Learning how to use sentence diagrams will enable you to strengthen your ability to identify parts of speech, make you aware of sentence structure, and show you how to use English more accurately. Once you have mastered the formula for diagramming, it is lots of fun to do.

The easiest sentence diagram shows a simple subject and a simple verb. To diagram this kind of sentence, you merely place the subject and the verb on a horizontal line separated by a crossing vertical line. For example:

1. Billy spoke.

Subject	Verb
Billy	spoke

2. Veronica was singing.

Subject	Verb
Veronica	was singing

3. Flowers bloom.

Subject	Verb
Flowers	bloom

4. We are finished.

Subject	Verb
We	are finished

Here are some clues to diagramming sentences. The *subject* will always be a *noun* (a person, place, or thing) or pronoun, and the *verb* will always be an *action* word (running, jumping, reading) or a *state of being* word (am, are, was, were).

Nouns	Pronouns	Verbs–action	Verbs–state of being
Grandma	I	twinkled	will be
Porsche™	we	nodded	might have been
Lake Erie	they	shake	seems
Chicago	he	fly	were
football	she	strum	am
guitar	it	catch	

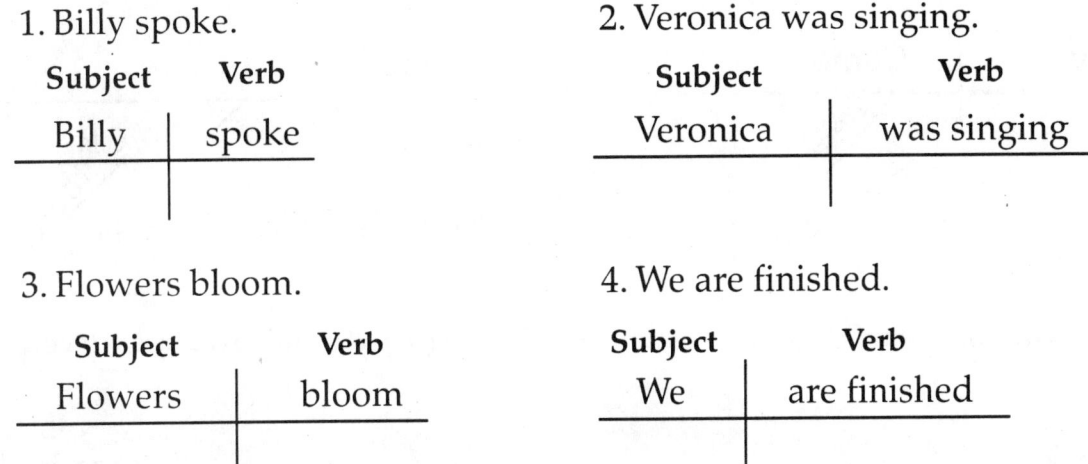

17

Copyright © 1994, Good Apple

GA1491

Sometimes the subject of the sentence is *understood* by the listener and, therefore, the subject's name is not mentioned in the sentence. Some examples of *you understood* sentences are shown below. Notice you could use the word *You* before each of these sentences. "You understood" sentences are diagrammed as follows:

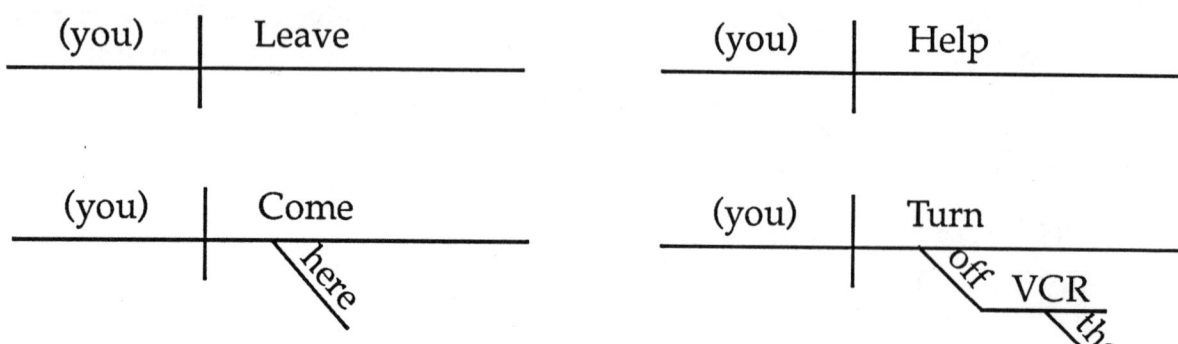

Notice that a sentence diagram shows the capital letters of a sentence but not the punctuation.

Here's how you would diagram a sentence with a *compound* (double) subject or verb.

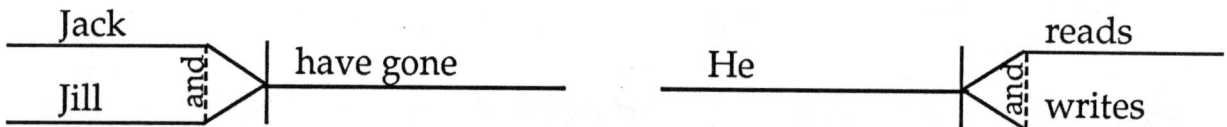

In some sentences, a noun or pronoun following a linking verb refers back to the subject. It is the same person or thing as the subject and can usually be interchanged with it. These nouns or pronouns are called *predicate nominatives*. Predicate nominatives rename the subject. This is how you would diagram a predicate nominative.

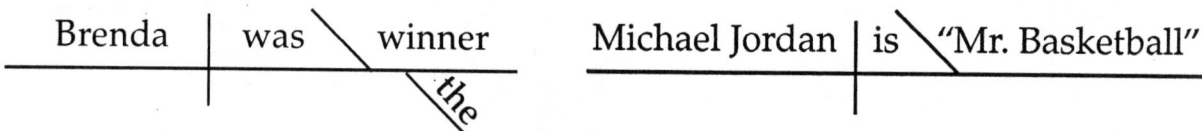

A *predicate adjective* is an adjective that follows a linking verb and modifies (changes or gives information about) the subject.

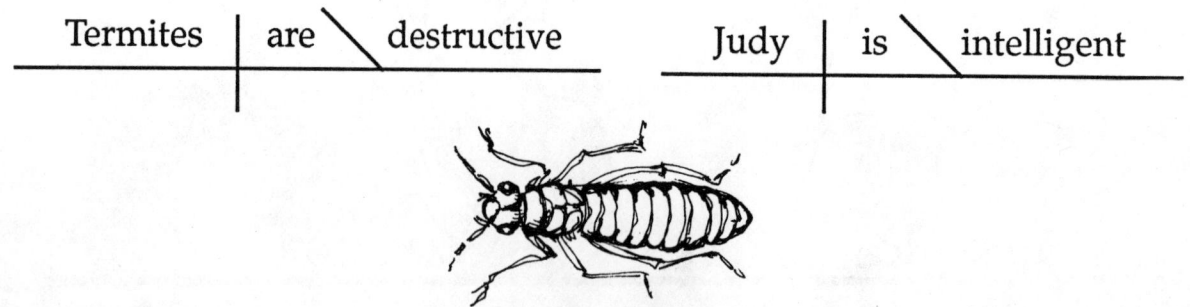

All sentences have a subject and a verb. Most sentences also have adjectives and adverbs. *Adjectives* modify (change or give information about) a noun or pronoun while *adverbs* modify (change or give information about) a verb, adjective, or another adverb. This is the way adjectives and adverbs are diagrammed.

Diagramming Adjectives

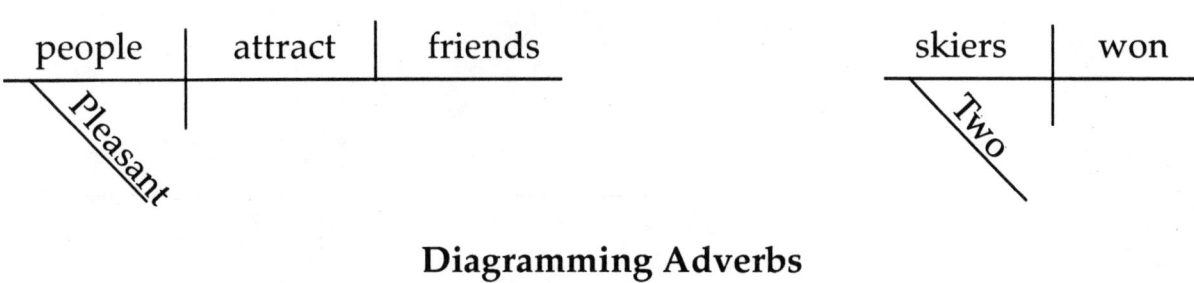

Diagramming Adverbs

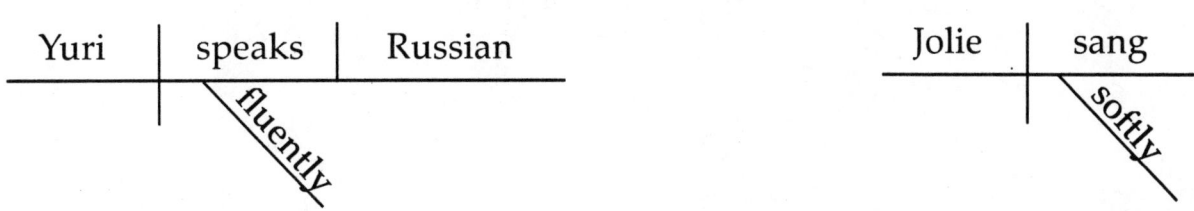

A *prepositional phrase* is a phrase starting with a preposition and is used to modify (change or give information about) other words. Some common prepositions are *to, at, in, on, up, by, for, from, with, under, over, above, between,* and *after*. The two kinds of prepositional phrases are adjective and adverb.

Adjective Prepositional Phrases

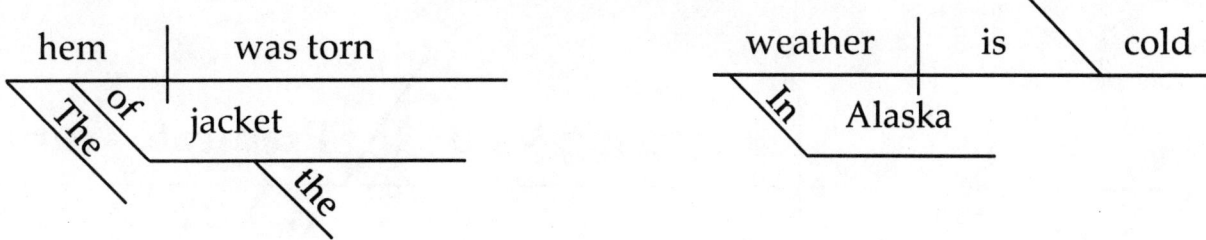

Adverb Prepositional Phrases

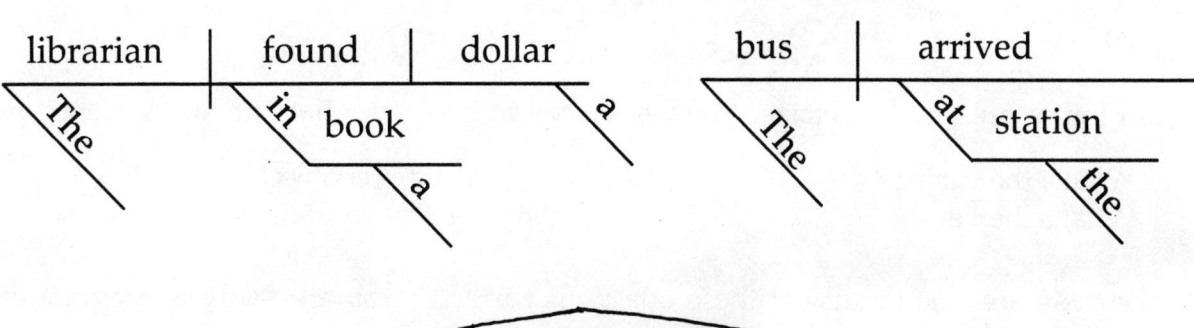

Your Diagramming Guide

Answers the question *who?* or *what?* Will be a noun or pronoun.	Is an action verb, action verb phrase, or state of being word or phrase.	Answers the question *whom?* or *what?* Will be a

Subject | Predicate | Direct Object

*Adjective / Prep. * Object / Adjective Phrase / Adjective*
*Adverb / Prep. * Object / Adverb Phrase / Adjective*
*Adjective / Prep. * Object / Adjective Phrase / Adjective*

* The *object* will be a noun or pronoun and will answer the question *whom?* or *what?* Note the *articles* (a, an, the) are always adjectives, so be sure to put them on an *adjective* line when you diagram any sentence.

Answers the question *who?* or *what?* Will be a noun or pronoun.	A verb which connects the subject to another word.	A noun, pronoun, or adjective which refers back to the subject.

Subject | Linking Verb | Predicate Word

Four important questions to ask yourself before you begin to diagram any sentence are:

What's the subject?   Is there a direct object?
What's the verb?   Are there any prepositional phrases?

When you are able to answer these questions correctly, you are ready to diagram any sentence, even complicated ones.

Eight Parts of Speech

Nouns are just the names of things.
As *birds* and *rice* and *snow* and *rings.*

Verbs are action words like *stir.*
Or *state* like *is* or *was* or *were.*

Adjectives describe a noun,
As *quacking* ducks and *pretty* gowns.

Prepositions precede a noun,
By, at, from, to, or *in* the town.

Pronouns take the place of nouns,
As *she* for woman, *they* for clowns.

Something is done; the *adverbs* then
tell *where* and *why* and *how* and *when.*
(how many)

And, or, and, *but* join words and clauses,
conjunctions used *instead of pauses.*

Strong feeling words are *Ouch!* and *Oh!*
They're *interjections, Ah! Bah!* and *Lo!*

Unknown

Where the words go when diagramming:

Straight Lines —————

1. Subject: nouns, pronouns

2. Predicates: action, state of being verbs

3. Objects: nouns, pronouns

4. Predicate words: nouns, pronouns, adjectives

Slanted Lines ⟋

1. Adjectives

2. Adverbs

3. Prepositions

Verb phrase equals the verb and helper (auxiliary).
Prepositional phrase is either adverbial or adjective and consists of a preposition and an object.

Now It's Your Turn
Diagramming Sentences

1. The sun is rising.

2. Return.

3. That story is a famous legend.

4. The tiny puppy waited outside the door.

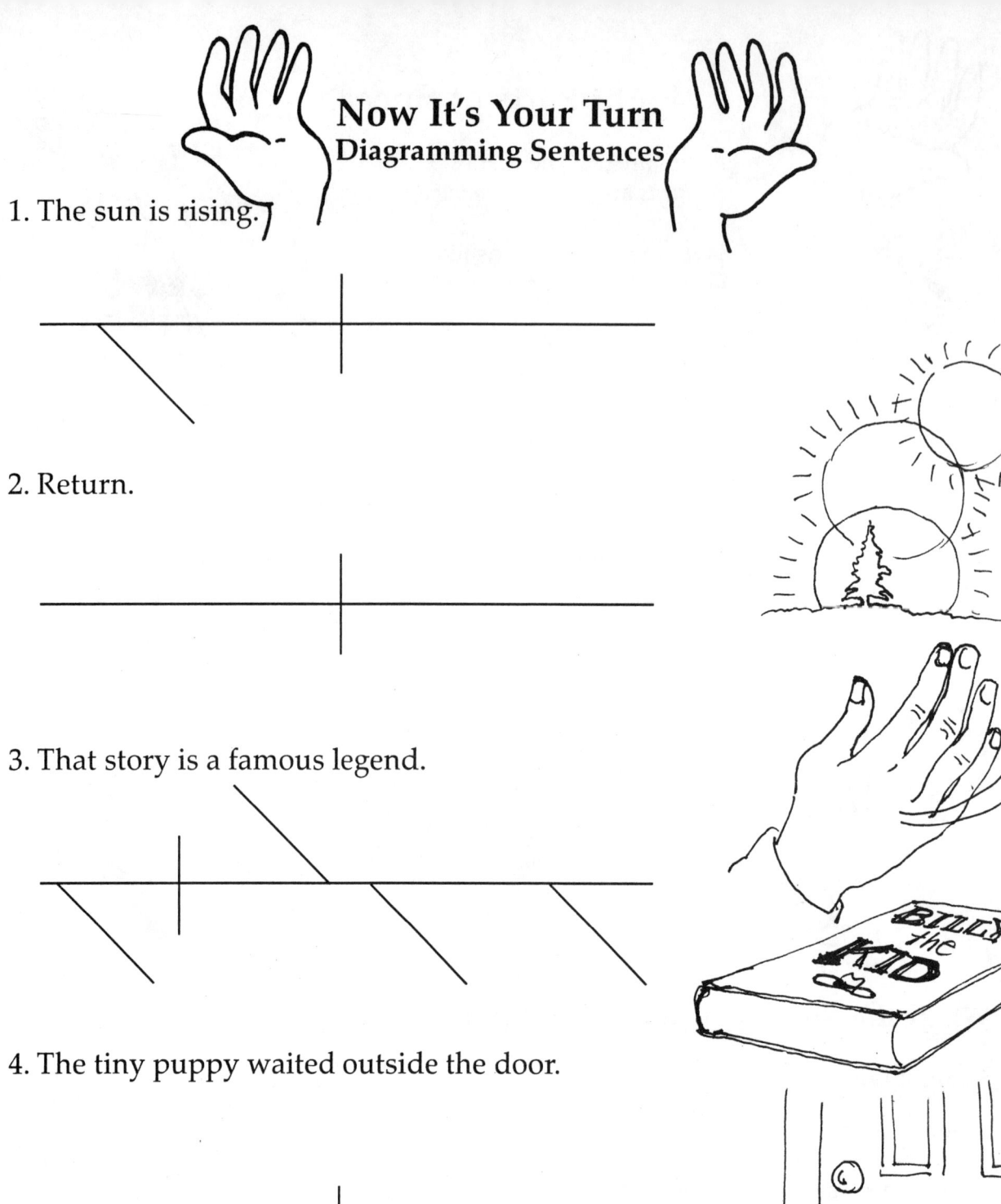

Copyright © 1994, Good Apple   GA1491

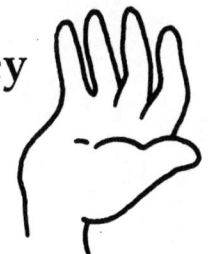 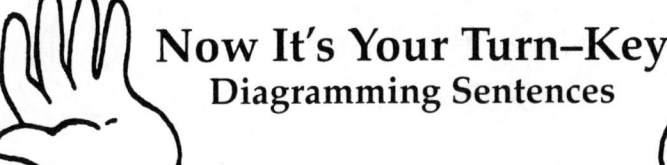

Now It's Your Turn–Key
Diagramming Sentences

1. The sun is rising.

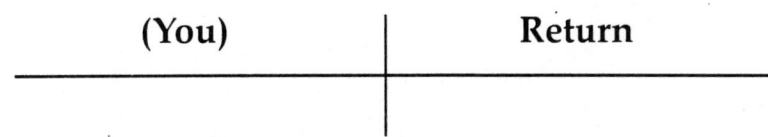

2. Return.

(You)	Return

3. That story is a famous legend.

4. The tiny puppy waited outside the door.

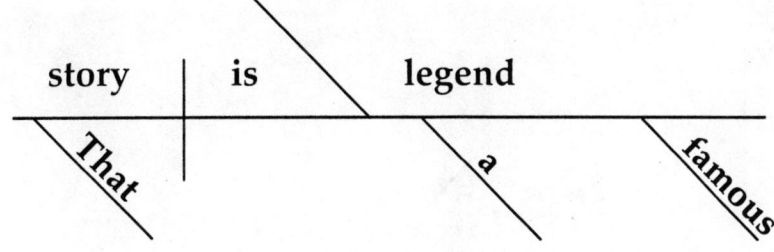

23

Now It's Your Turn
Diagramming Sentences

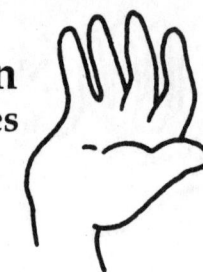

5. This stew tastes strange.

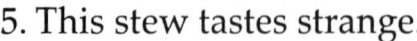

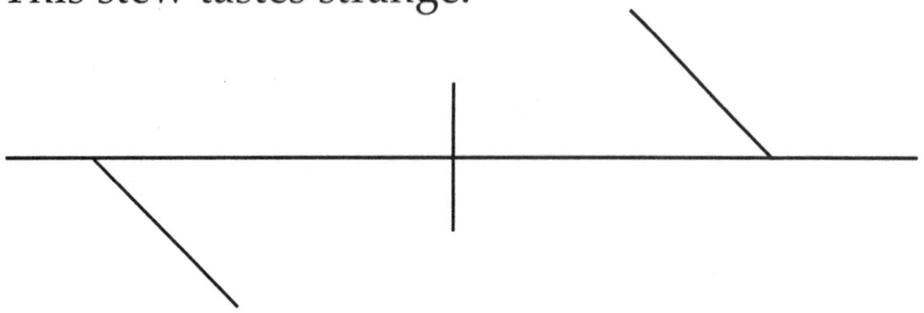

6. Wait!

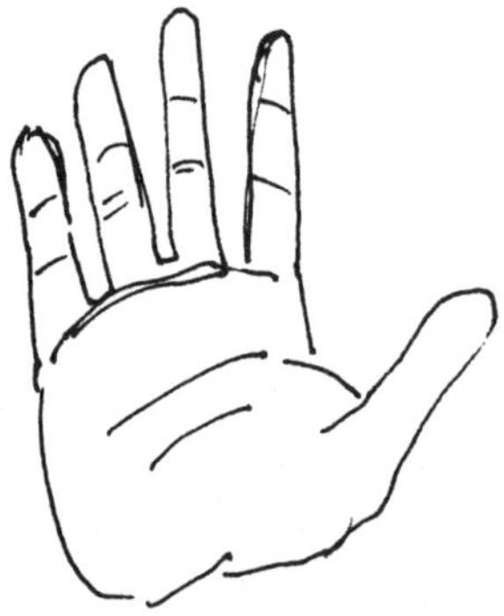

7. That old clock has never worked.

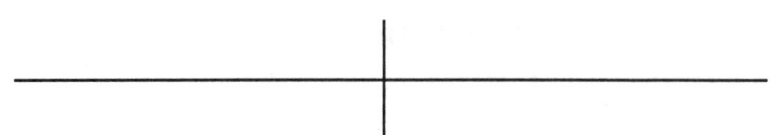

8. We listened to music on our new stereo.

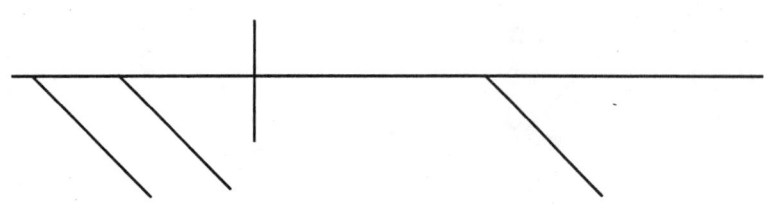

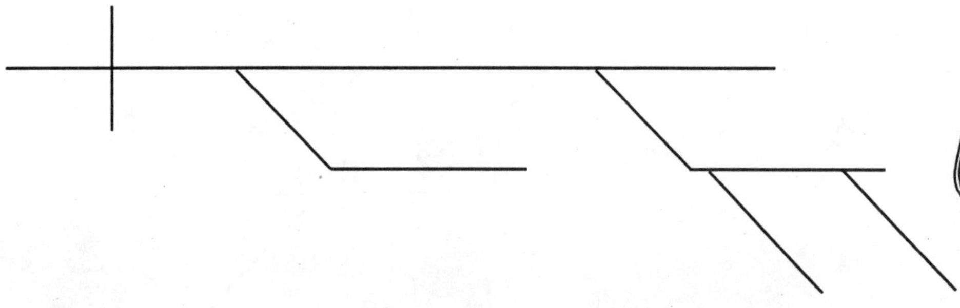

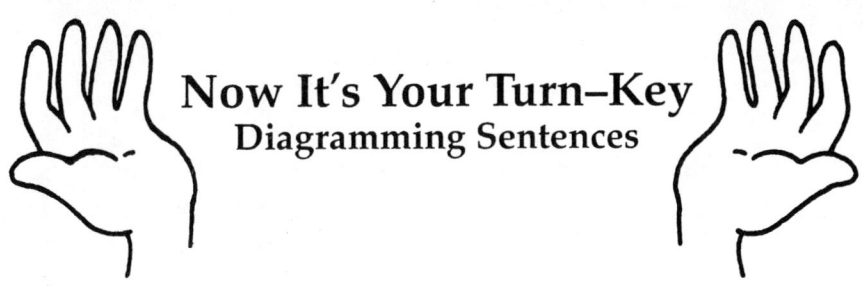

Now It's Your Turn–Key
Diagramming Sentences

5. This stew tastes strange.

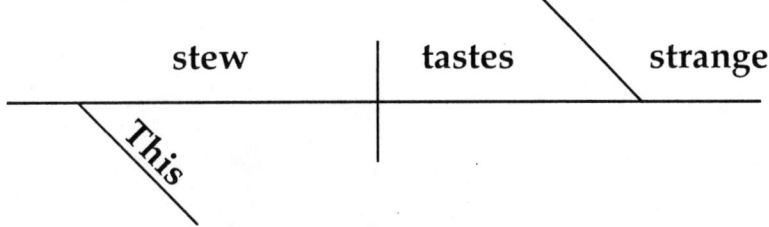

6. Wait!

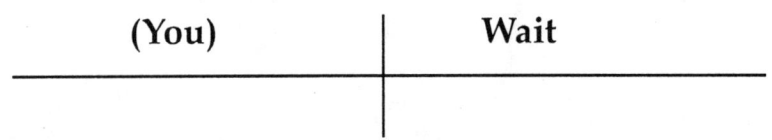

7. That old clock has never worked.

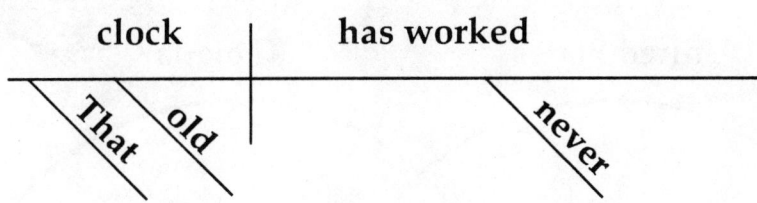

8. We listened to music on our new stereo.

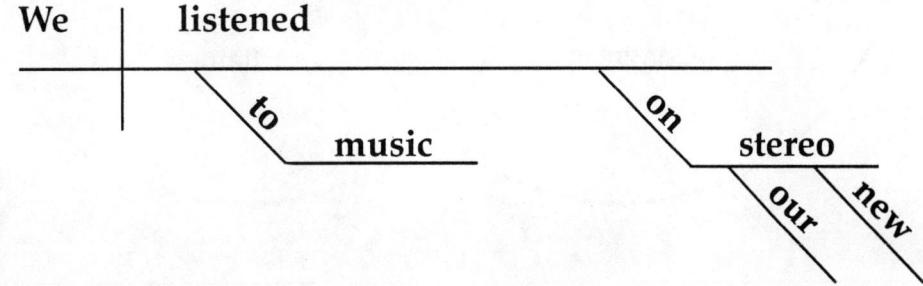

Venn Diagrams

A Venn diagram is a technique for classifying likenesses and differences. It is formed by two overlapping circles. The center part of the circles indicates likenesses; the outside parts indicate differences. A Venn diagram is a useful way for thinking and/or writing about comparisons. Listed below are two examples of Venn diagrams. One is for science, the other one is for social studies. Venn diagrams can be used to compare any topics. On the next page create your own Venn diagrams.

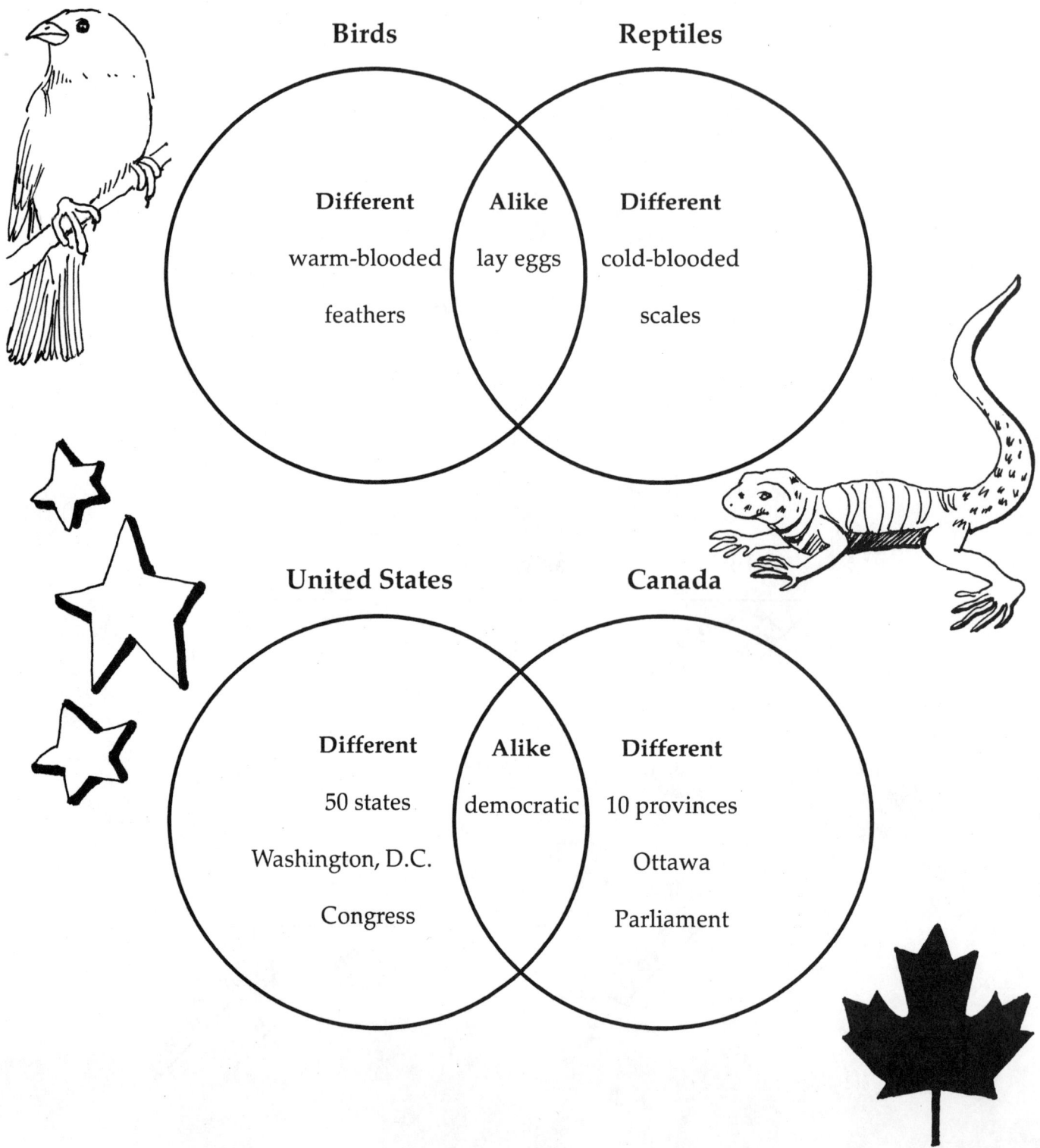

Birds — Reptiles

Different
warm-blooded
feathers

Alike
lay eggs

Different
cold-blooded
scales

United States — Canada

Different
50 states
Washington, D.C.
Congress

Alike
democratic

Different
10 provinces
Ottawa
Parliament

Copyright © 1994, Good Apple

26

GA1491

Writing, Writing, Writing

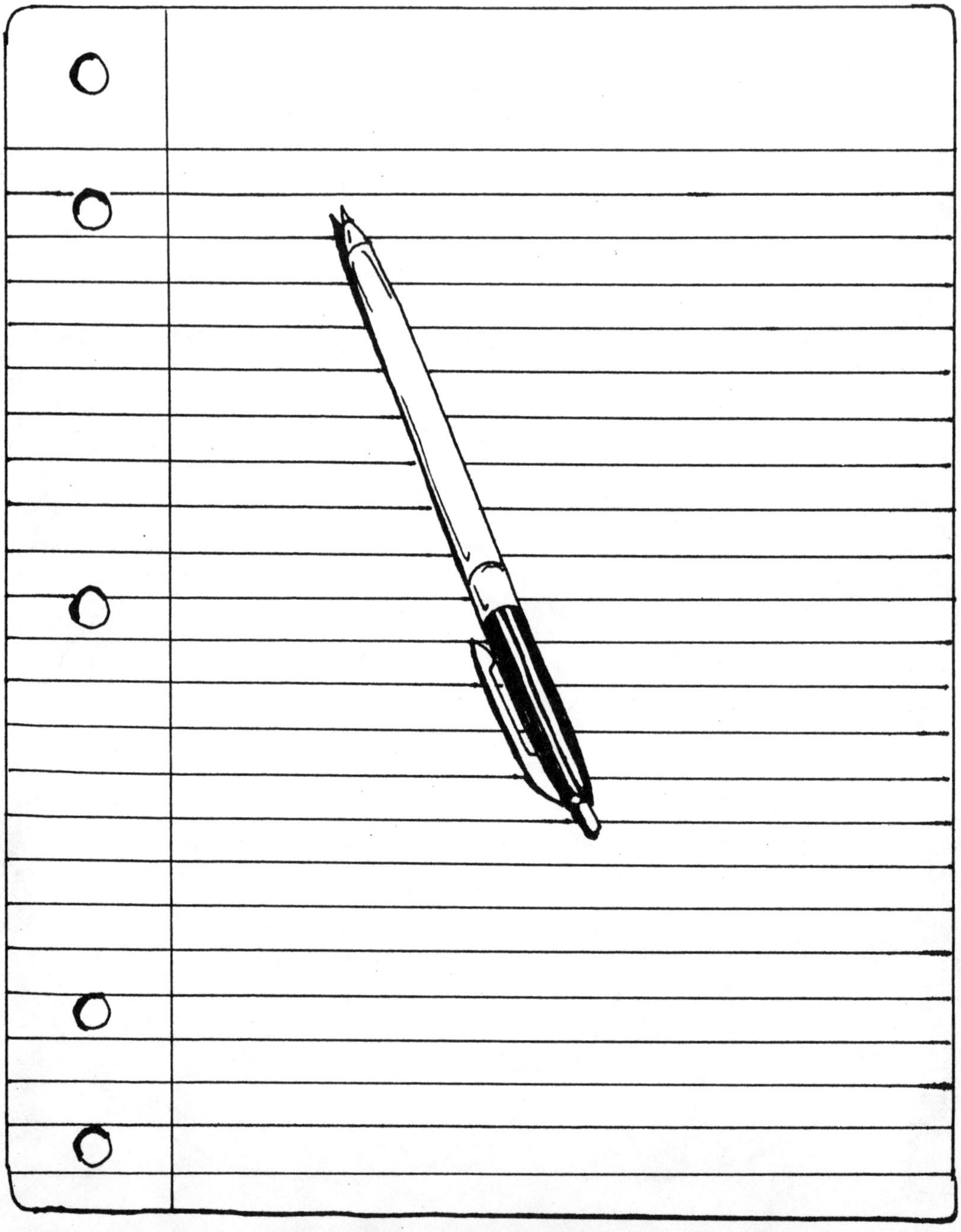

The Web of Writing

The best way to begin any writing project is to free your mind, opening it to thoughts, ideas, memories, terms, and phrases. To assist you in writing your "first impressions," it is a good idea to use a writing *web*. A web is also called brainstorming or mapping. Whatever term is used, the purpose is the same. It is to provide you with an effective tool for creative thinking to enable you to remove the "shackles" of narrow-minded thinking.

A sample web is provided to show you how to generate ideas for writing. In the center circle, you may list the topic you want to write about; then you will fill the other circles with ideas that freely "pop" into your head when you think about that topic. This isn't the time to judge the merits of your ideas; it isn't the time to concern yourself with how good your thoughts are. It is the time to write free of censorship. The purpose is to write a "shopping list of the mind"–words, ideas, images, memories. This is the time to do free writing.

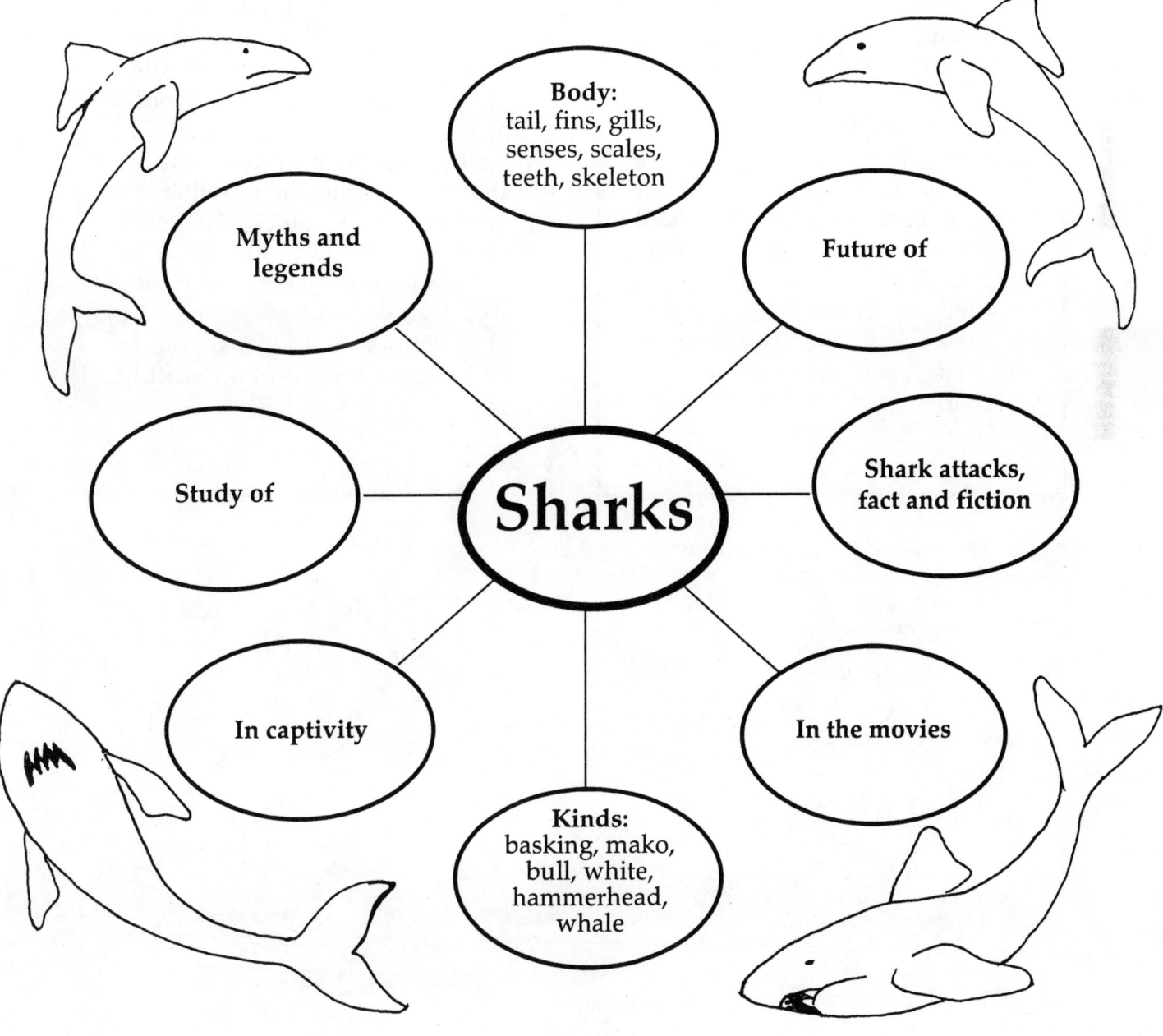

The Writing Process

Writing, like cooking, is a process. No two people cook alike, no two people write alike; however, writers agree that there are certain necessary steps that all writers follow in order to produce a well-composed piece of writing. Some writers claim that there are four steps in the process, but other writers say that there are five steps. The number of steps is not important; the process used by writers is. Following the steps of writing makes writing manageable. Use the flowchart to assist you in the writing process.

*Stage One: Prewriting

Prewriting is the planning stage of writing. It is the time when the writer gathers ideas, feelings, thoughts, and experiences to begin the writing process. This is the time when the writer talks to other writers to get their input and to establish a purpose, focus, and audience for what the writer plans to write. This is the stage where the writer makes use of a writing web, map, or brainstorming chart. It is a time when the writer may find exploring ideas with others, reading, and researching a variety of topics useful. Once a topic is selected, it needs to be given focus and form.

Stage Two: First Draft

Writing the first draft provides the writer with a palette to begin a "painting." This is the stage to concentrate on the free flow of ideas, the time to think on paper without regard for spelling, grammar, or handwriting. At this time the writer is free to let the words, phrases, or sentences flow. The writer may use abbreviations, shorthand notes, or drawings to express ideas as quickly as possible. It is the time when the writer gets to experiment with words, style, voice, and meaning. The draft should be double-spaced to make later revision and editing easier.

* See "The Web of Writing" activity on page 29.

Stage Three: "Cooking" and Conferencing

Once the writer has written a first draft, the piece of writing should be set aside to "cook," to "simmer," just as a good cook sets aside a pot of soup or a container of stew in order to let the spices seep into all the ingredients. Then the writer goes back to the piece and begins the revision process. This may be done by sharing the draft with peers, by reading the draft to a friend, or by the writer rereading the draft and adding new ideas, noting the paper's strengths and weaknesses, and asking others or oneself questions regarding the effectiveness of the piece of writing.

Stage Four: Proofreading, Revising, and Editing

Now the writer gets serious about the final outcome of the piece. The writer must focus on order, clarity, and specific details. The paper's beginning, middle, and ending must be examined to be sure that they are appropriate to do their job of introduction, development, and conclusion. Word choices must be scrutinized to be certain that they are the best they can be for the task they perform. Spelling, grammar, usage, and mechanics must be inspected to make certain the paper is as error-free as possible. This is the stage in which the paper is "polished to perfection." A final, clean, correct copy is now made.

Stage Five: Publishing and Sharing

Publishing and sharing can take many forms. The writer may choose to make an oral presentation, display the writing on a classroom bulletin board, put it in the writing center for all to see, or read it to friends or family members. The writer may also wish to share the writing with a larger audience and submit the writing for formal publication in an anthology, the school newspaper, or student writing contest. This is the stage in which the writer feels a true sense of accomplishment, a sense that writing and all the work involved in the writing process is indeed worthwhile.

Now It's Your Turn
*Stage One:
Prewriting Webbing

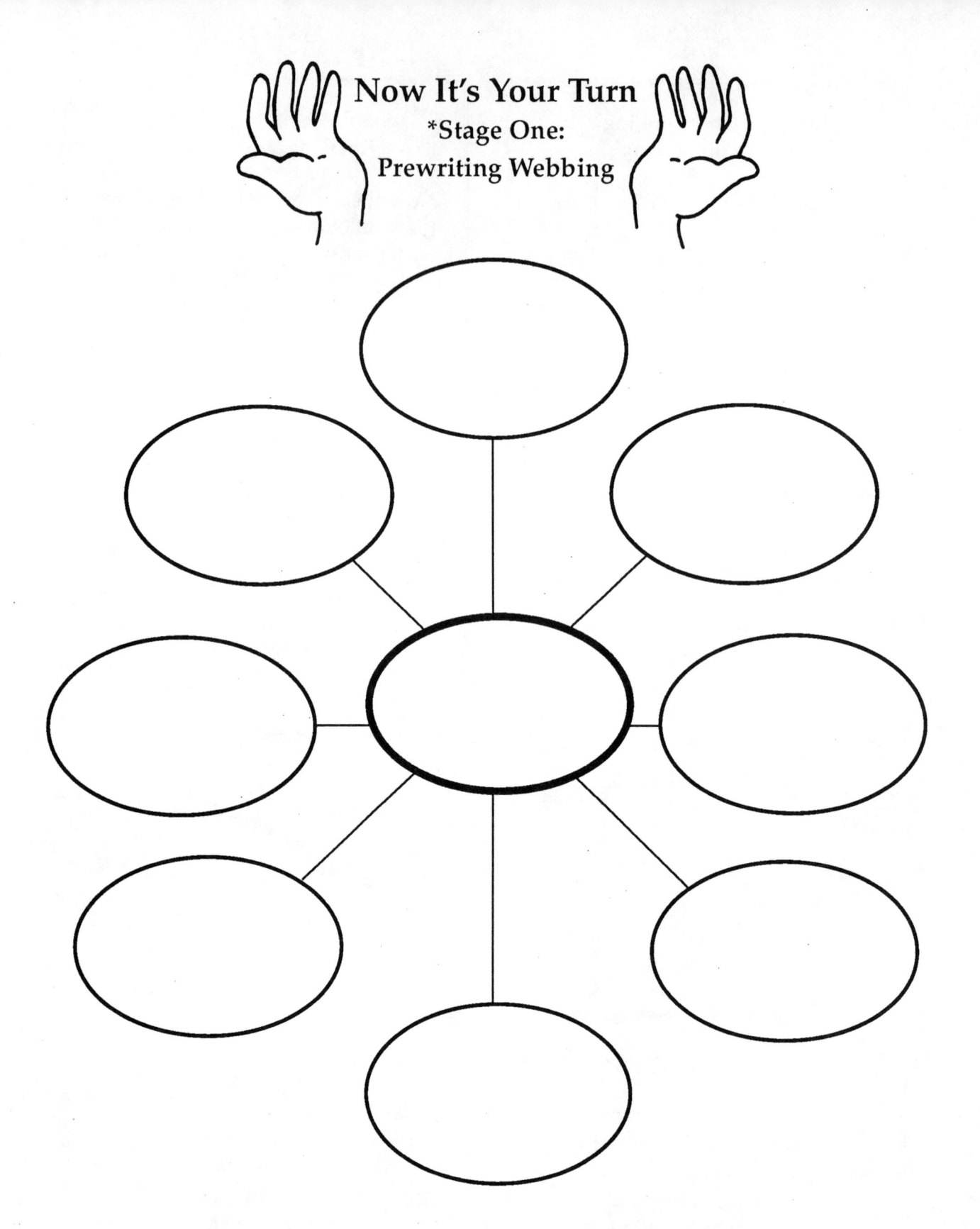

Now It's Your Turn

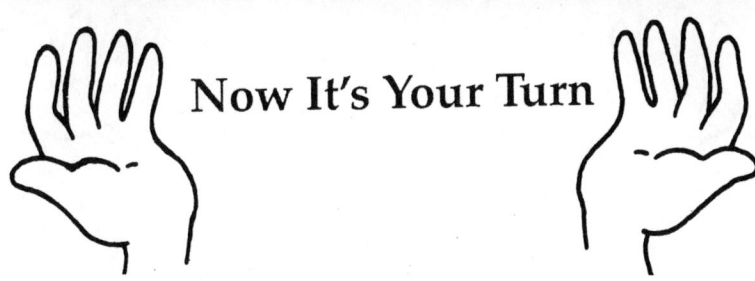

* Stage Two: First Draft

* Use The Web of Writing for your brainstorming work and use the grid for your first draft.

Now It's Your Turn

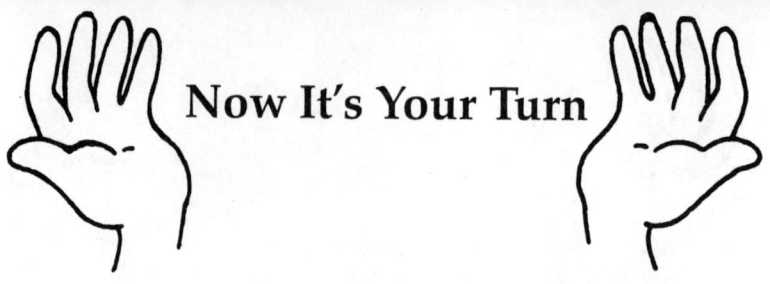

* **Stage Three: "Cooking" and Conferencing**

Stage Four: Proofreading, Revising, and Editing

* Use this page for revising and editing your writing.

Now It's Your Turn

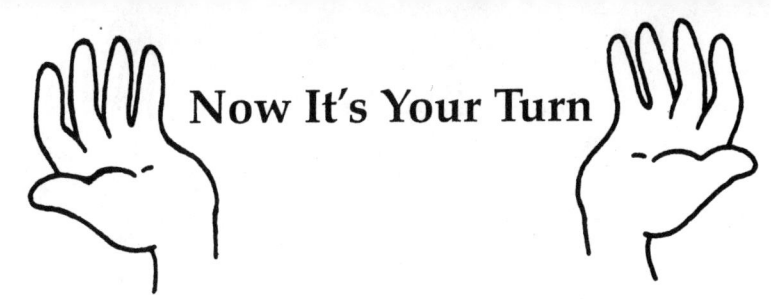

Stage Five: Publishing and Sharing

Now It's Your Turn

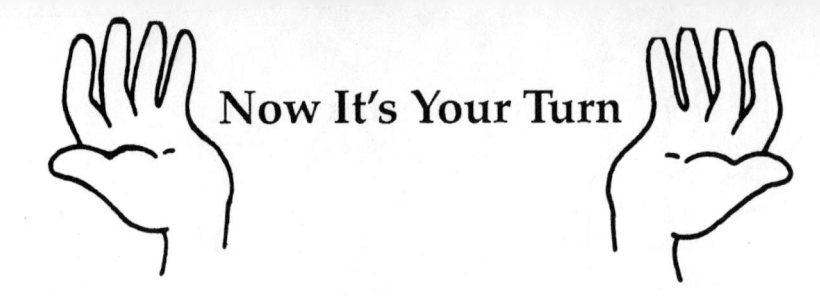

Stage Five: Publishing and Sharing (cont'd.)

Now It's Your Turn

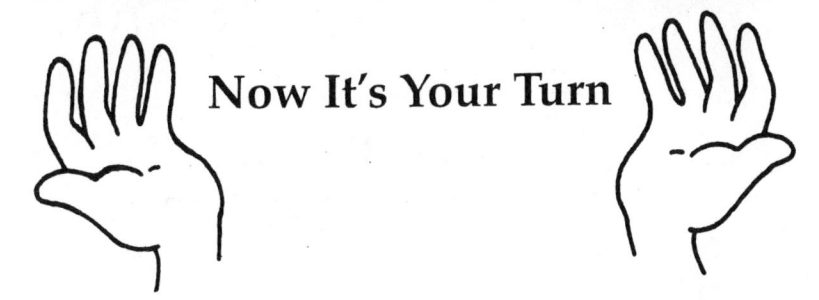

Stage Five: Publishing and Sharing

A Poster and Paper

THE HISTORY OF ROCK MUSIC

A Photo Essay

Sharks

One of the most awesome creatures of the earth is the shark.

From the beginning of time, men have recorded their fear of sharks in myths.

An Anthology, Book, or Newspaper Article

A Writing Contest

Narrative Writing
The Art of Storytelling

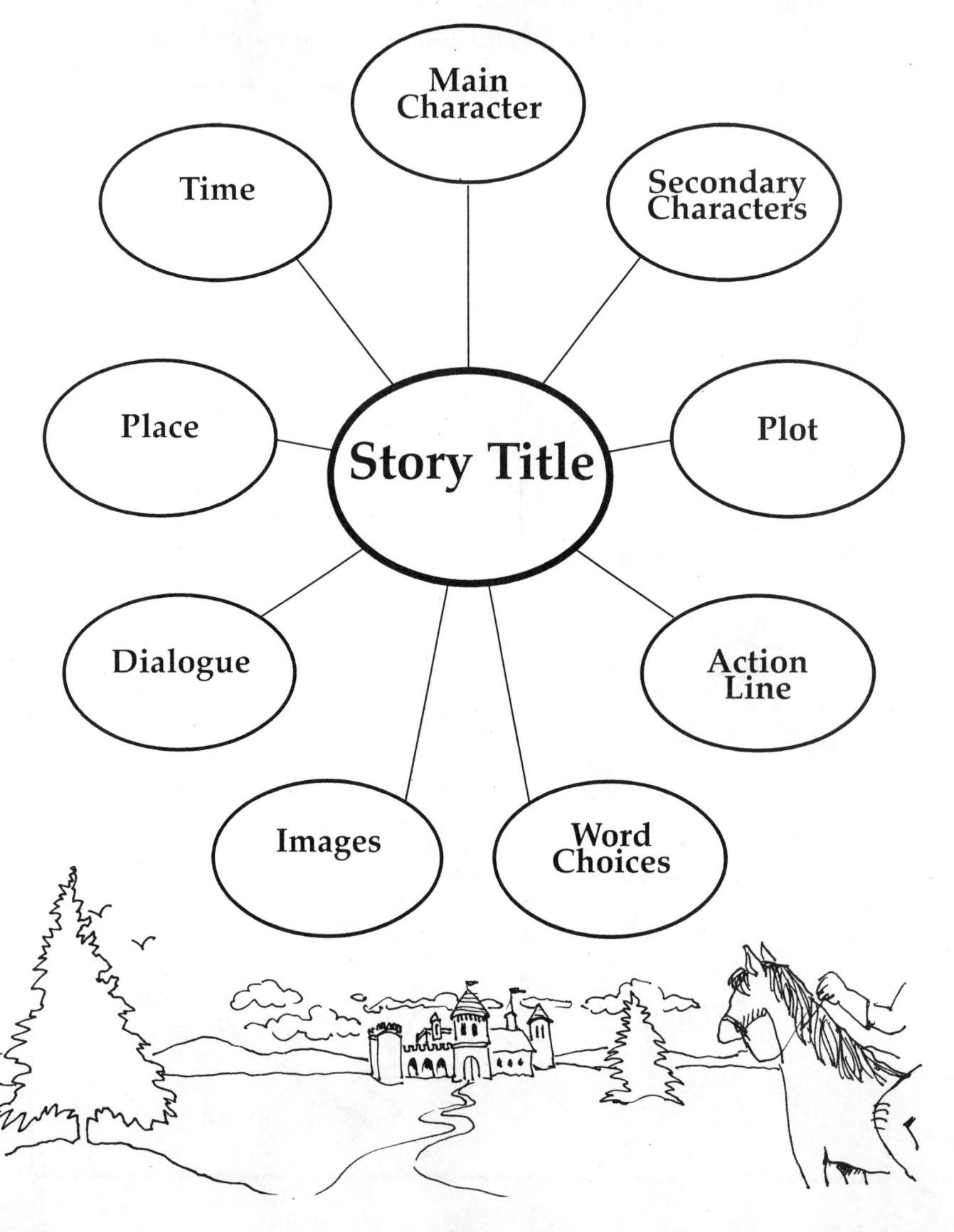

- Main Character
- Secondary Characters
- Plot
- Action Line
- Word Choices
- Images
- Dialogue
- Place
- Time

Story Title

Narrative Writing
The Art of Storytelling

Everyone likes a good story. In ancient Greece and Rome; in Egypt, India, and China; in castles of kings and knights, all over the world there have lived magnificent storytellers. They plied their craft, told their tales, recorded fact and fiction, and have left us a wealth of tales which are still enjoyed today.

Narrative writing is writing that tells a *story*. It can be real or imagined. All that is essential is that the story have a good *plot*. The story may be about pillaging pirates, animated animals, or futuristic inhabitants of earth. A good story demands that the plot is resolved in an acceptable way. Without an intriguing plot and its resolution, there is no story, there is nothing the reader will find worthy of reading.

The *conflict* or problem in the story might be between two people (friends now enemies), between an individual and nature (being caught in a dust storm or hurricane), or within the main *character* (who has a difficult choice to make). Conflict adds drama, excitement, and a reason for readers to read the story. In addition to an engaging problem, the story must have a satisfactory ending (but not necessarily where all the characters "live happily ever after"). It is only important that the resolution of the conflict be interesting and believable.

A story, as you know, tells of a happening. It has a *beginning*, which includes an introduction of the characters and a setting (time and place in which the story occurs). The beginning of your story deals with the three W's: who, when, and where. It is the foundation of the *narrative*.

After the characters and setting have been introduced, the reader sits back and watches the plot develop. This is the exciting or *middle* part of the story where the action takes place. Often a writer will use clue words to alert the reader to the action which is about to begin. For example, the writer may start a paragraph with *suddenly, all of a sudden, all at once,* or *just then*. Jack London uses this technique in his book, *The Call of the Wild*: "And then, suddenly, without warning, uttering a cry that was inarticulate and more the cry of an animal, John Thorton sprang upon the man who wielded the club. Hal was hurled backwards, as though struck by a falling tree."

The middle or action part of the story has two roles: to begin the action of the story and to arouse the reader's curiosity. This part is followed by the third part of the story or the climax. The *climax* is the part that tells what happens in the story. The climax might solve a mystery, expose a riddle, or resolve a conflict. If a story fails to have a climax, the reader feels disgruntled, disappointed, and frustrated. The climax is the heart of the story; its job is to unlock the story's intrigue. It must be carefully crafted and convincingly conveyed.

The fourth and final part of a story is the *ending*. It may be abrupt or drawn out a bit. But its task is to bring the story to an appropriate conclusion. With the end, the story action is complete, the mystery is unraveled, the characters have changed during the course of the story.

The *title* of the story is also important. It is the bait needed to hook the reader. It should be a key to the story and fit it well. But the title should not give away the plot line because if it does, the reader won't read beyond the title. Clever writers devise clever titles for their narratives.

Irresistible Beginnings and Endings

The most important part of what you write is the beginning. Your opening page, paragraph, or words must *capture* the *attention* of your reader immediately and compel the reader to keep on reading; otherwise your piece is doomed. How many times have you picked up a book or magazine, started reading, gotten bored, and abandoned the material? That is precisely what you don't want your reader to do. There is no specific way to grab a reader. You can begin with humor, surprise, or a fresh approach. Each technique has the potential to entice a reader. Beginnings are known as *leads* in the world of professional writing, and when we think about a movie or video, the *lead* is the most important person, or the person the audience pays to see or hear.

Once you have the reader's attention, you must hold it. You must "build your case" if you want the reader to go on reading to the end. Your beginning should give the reader the feeling that he or she is going on a thrilling roller coaster ride. It should create the anticipation you feel right after being strapped in your seat on a roller coaster, knowing that an exciting ride is soon to begin.

The next most important part of your piece of writing is the end. When do you finish? How do you finish? Have you left the reader with a sense of being comfortable with the conclusion? These are questions you need to address as a writer. In fact, you must take as much care ending your piece of writing as you did beginning it.

One way to learn how to write powerful beginnings and memorable endings is to examine, explore, and emulate what the pros do to "hook" us. Here are three provocative *beginnings* from well-known, contemporary writers of fiction and nonfiction.

Fiction

- **S. E. Hinton**, *The Outsiders*. "When I stepped out into the bright sunlight from the darkness of the movie house, I had only two things on my mind: Paul Newman and a ride home."

- **Scott O'Dell**, *Island of the Blue Dolphins*. "I remember the day the Aleut ships came to our island. At first it seemed like a small shell afloat on the sea. Then it grew larger and was a gull with folded wings. At last in the rising sun it became what it really was–a red ship with two red sails."

- **Katherine Paterson**, *Bridge to Terabithia*. "Ba-room, ba-room, ba-room, baripity, baripity, baripity, baripity. Good. His dad had the pickup going."

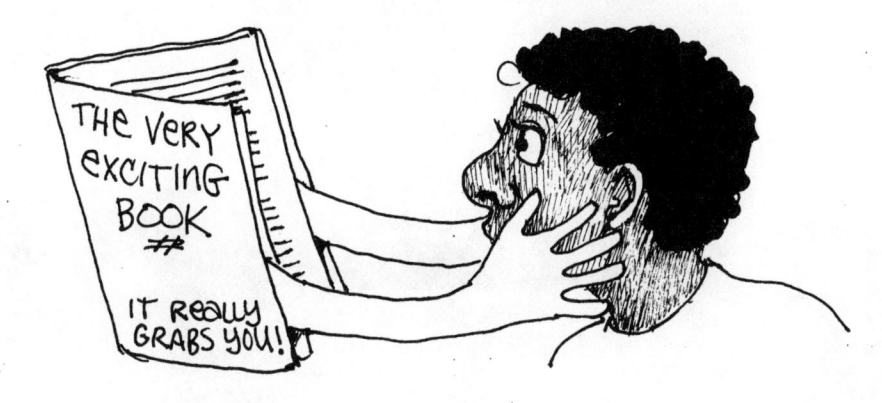

Nonfiction

- **Isaac Asimov**, *Words from the Myths*. "Human beings wouldn't be human if they didn't wonder about the world about them. Many thousands of years ago, when mankind was still primitive, men must have looked out of caves and wondered about what they saw."

- **Jane Yolen**, *Simple Gifts*. "The house is like other New England houses, plain and sturdy. It is large, well built, with fireplaces in each of the rooms; for the owner is a man of means. But the house differs from the other houses in the village because it is no longer just a house."

- **Alvin and Virginia Silverstein**, *Cats: All About Them*. "When we moved from the city to our home in the country, some acquaintances bought us a traditional house gift: two kittens."

Students can also write alluring beginnings. Here are three examples of fiction and nonfiction (from school reports).

Fiction

- **Melissa Wieland**. "As I closed the screen door, I looked out through the stand of white birch, onto the murky, green lake and was overcome by grief."

- **Heather Brooks**. "'No. Really, Mom. I don't want to go,' Elizabeth yelled as she glared at her mother. There was no doubt that this wasn't going to be an ordinary day."

- **Dan McQuade**. "'Let's get out of here, or we're sure to be killed', said Dash. 'Hadn't he warned his pal often enough of the dangers lurking so late at night in this part of the city?' wondered Dash."

Nonfiction

- **Christin Luckman**. "Speed skiing is a relatively new demonstration sport in this year's Olympic Games at Albertville. It is often confused with downhill, but speed skiing is a sport of smooth sailing, straight down a fast-paced track."

- **Brian Faber**. "Freestyle skiing is one of the Olympic sports that draws huge crowds whenever the event takes place."

- **Courtney Murdock**. "What is the sport of biathlon? What is a biathlon course like? What rules govern biathlon competition? How is biathlon scored?"

Now let's investigate well-written *endings*. First the pros.

Fiction

- **Sylvia Cassedy**, *Behind the Attic Wall*. "'What other one?' Maggie's head spun back and forth. 'Who?' and her eye swept across the room. There was an extra chair at the table, she now noticed, and strangely a third bed. Other things, too, seemed added, rearranged, and she let out a quick gasp as she caught sight of something else in the corner: a small round bowler, its crown looking as though it had just been brushed with the sleeve of a coat, hanging on the clothes hook; and, against the wall, a small walking stick, its silver knob shining like a smooth, perfect moon."

- **E.B. White**, *The Trumpet of the Swan*. "Sam put his notebook away. He undressed himself and slid into bed. He lay there, wondering what *crepuscular* meant. In less than three minutes he was fast asleep." (Second to last paragraph in the book)

- **Ray Bradbury**, *The Illustrated Man*. "I ran down the road in the moonlight. I didn't look back. A small town lay ahead and asleep. I knew that, long before morning, I would reach the town . . . ."

Now the student-written endings.

Nonfiction

- **John Fearncombe**. "After solving what is now known as the 'Screaming Woman Case,' I could not figure out why the ex-husband would get so angry, but then again, this was Chicago."

- **Kent Legel**. "Chung Lee could see the outlines of the New York skyscrapers. All at once and without any warning, he began to shout, 'I'm free, I'm free, I'm free,' and he began dancing wildly on the deck of the ship that had taken him from oppression in China to freedom in America."

- **Adrienne White**. "That is the main difference between Meredith and me; I take the time to smell the flowers, and she walks past them because she doesn't need to think about them."

Because the emphasis here has been on eloquent beginnings and soul-satisfying endings, this does not mean that as a writer you can ignore the middle of your fiction or nonfiction pieces. Of course, it goes without saying that all the parts must work together as a well-assembled roller coaster ride. Keep in mind that some writing sings, while other writing hits a note of sour discord. As a writer, you need to train your ear to recognize the sound of melodic writing, whether it is yours, another student's, or one of the pros'.

Writers need to write.

Now It's Your Turn

My Beginnings and My Endings

1. Write three beginnings.

   a. _____
   _____
   _____

   b. _____
   _____
   _____

   c. _____
   _____
   _____

2. Write three endings.

   a. _____
   _____
   _____

   b. _____
   _____
   _____

   c. _____
   _____
   _____

ABC ★ XYZ

Now It's Your Turn

To help you get started with writing a narrative, here are some suggestions that might "trigger" a story for you. Keep in mind those essential ingredients for any story.

1. *Character* means the people in the story. Who are they? What are they like? What are they doing? What do they want? And by the end of the story, we want to see how they have changed.

2. *Setting* means the place in which the story takes place. Where is it? What is it like? What effect does it have on the characters? For example, if the setting is Hawaii, this will have a different effect on the characters than if the setting were Alaska. Settings affect food and clothing, outlook and attitude, and so much more.

3. What is the struggle, conflict, or problem in the story? The plot is usually brought about because of something the character or characters in the story want and are willing to do anything to get. Conflict in stories centers around four types. They are:

   - **Person vs. Self**—The struggle is within the mind or conscience of the individual as he or she struggles to make a personal decision. Some examples include: Should you cheat on a test when no one will know? Should you go against your parents' wishes because your friends want you to? Should you make friends with someone no one else likes?

   - **Person vs. Nature**—The struggle is against outside forces such as floods, earthquakes, hurricanes, or any natural disaster. This also includes struggle against any beasts of the earth — insects, reptiles, apes, etc.

   - **Person vs. Society**—The struggle is against social forces outside the individual. It includes the fight for justice against injustice, the conflict between prejudice and loss of freedom, the battle between the individual and another individual.

   - **Person vs. the Supernatural**—The struggle is against God or gods (as seen in myths and legends) or against evil spirits like the devil (as seen in the classic story "The Devil and Daniel Webster").

Characters	Settings	Conflicts
parents	at a rock concert	lost money
siblings	at the beach	parents aren't home
friends	at the mall	broken arm
kids at school	in the locker room	lights go out
animal(s)	in the rain forest	scary, unfamiliar sounds

Now It's Your Turn

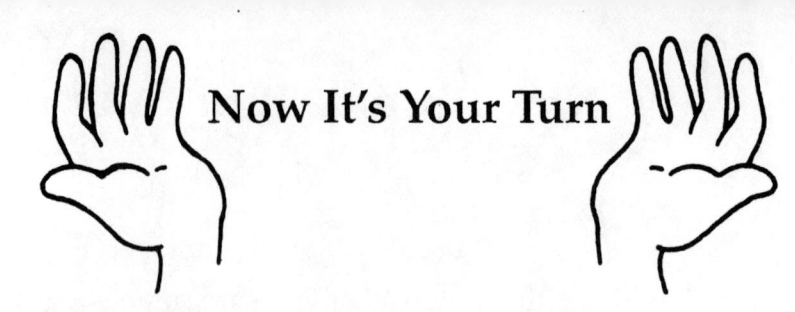

1. Title _____

2. Plot (sequence of events in the story) _____

_____
_____
_____
_____
_____
_____
_____
_____
_____
_____
_____
_____

3. Conflict (collision of thoughts, feelings, actions, values, or persons in the story)

_____
_____
_____
_____
_____

4. Characters (persons or animals who are central to the story). Write physical and psychological descriptions.

   a. Main character

   _____
   _____
   _____
   _____
   _____
   _____
   _____
   _____

   b. Supporting characters. Write their physical and psychological descriptions.

   _____
   _____
   _____
   _____
   _____
   _____
   _____
   _____

5. Setting. Clearly outline the following:

   a. Time _____

   b. Place _____

Now It's Your Turn

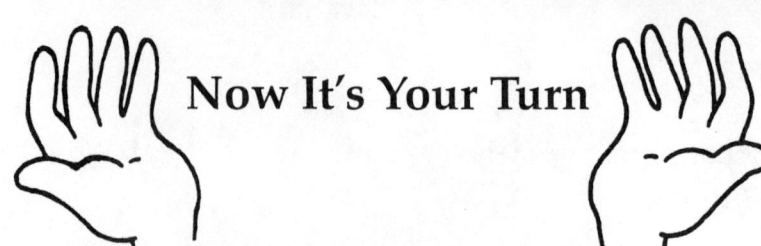

My Story

Now It's Your Turn

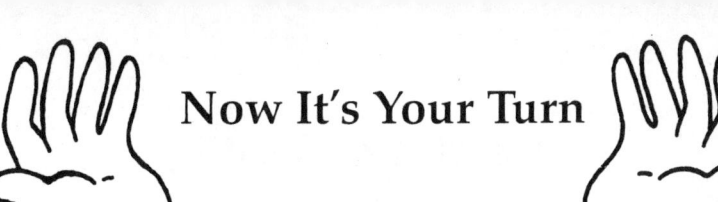

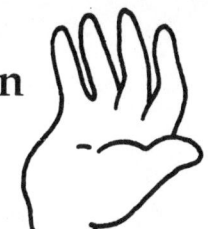

My Story (cont'd.)

Descriptive Writing

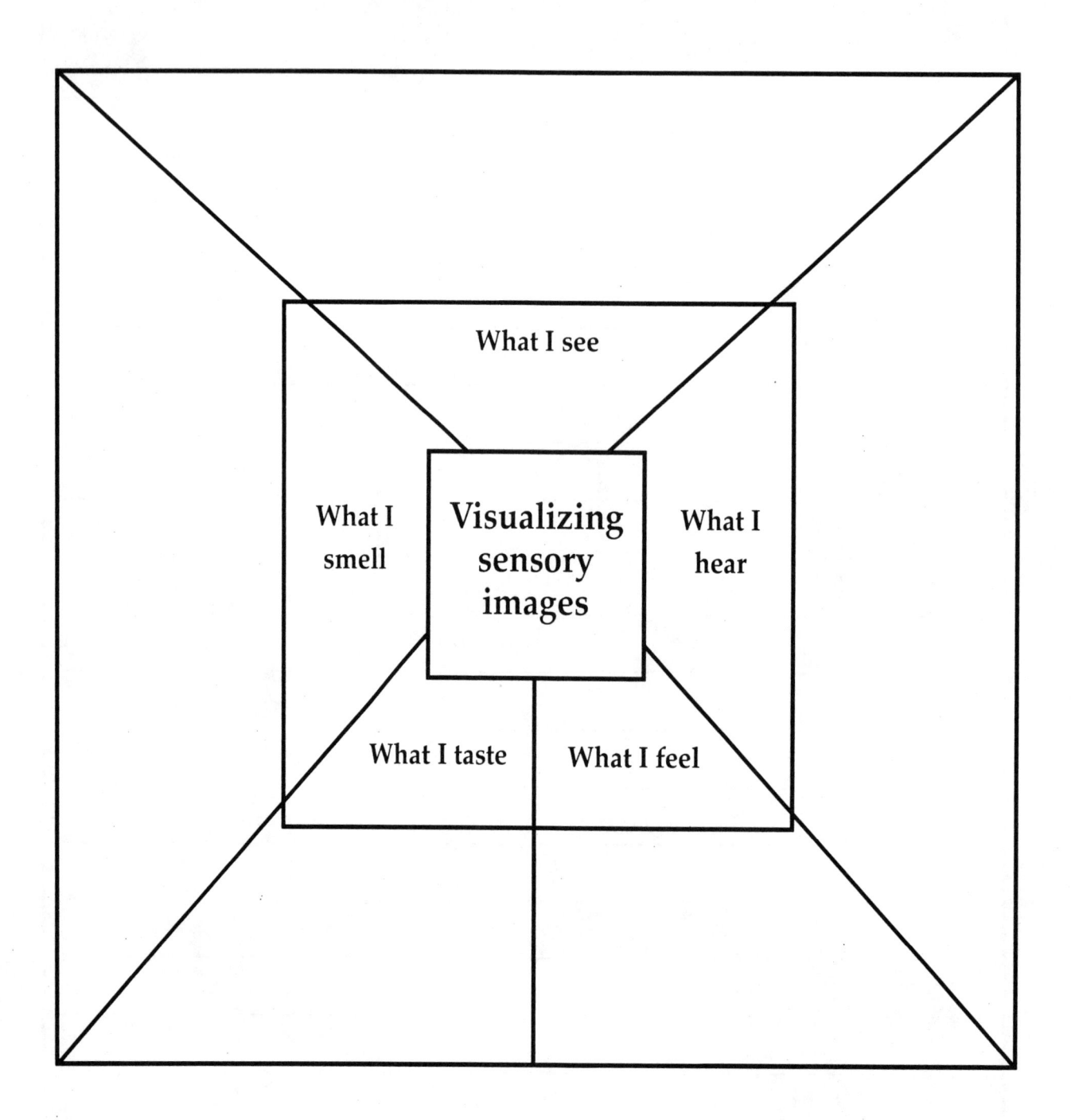

What I see

What I smell

Visualizing sensory images

What I hear

What I taste

What I feel

Descriptive Writing

In writing good descriptive paragraphs, essays, and themes, you must decide what your focus is and what impression you want to leave with your reader. It is your task to choose your words carefully, select precise details, and appeal to the reader's senses. In addition, your descriptive writing must flow smoothly so that the reader sees the "word-pictures" you are creating in his or her mind. In order to write a descriptive piece, there are guidelines to follow. When describing a person you must strive to capture the essence of the person, not merely list the person's physical characteristics. If you describe the person only on a surface level, the result will be like reading a police report on a missing person: it will not make the person "come alive" for the reader. A good method to give your characters personality is to show your audience who they are by their actions. The author Sterling North shows you how to do this in his description of Rascal, the main character in his novel by the same name.

> Rascal was a demon for speed. Weighing two pounds at most, this absurd and lovable creature had the heart of a lion. He had learned to stand in the closely woven wire [bicycle] basket with his feet wide apart and his hands *firmly gripping the front rim, his small button of a nose pointed straight into the wind, and his ringtail streaming back like the plume of a hunting dog* that has come to a point. The most amusing aspect of his racing costume was his *natural black goggles* around his bright eyes making him look like Barney Oldfield [a race-car driver] coming down the homestretch.

Notice how the italicized words used by North make it easy and enjoyable for the reader to picture Rascal sitting in the basket of Sterling's bike as the two head into town on a sunny, summer afternoon. It is quite clear to the reader what is happening in the scene because the author uses words that appeal to the reader's sense of sight, sound, smell, taste, and touch. That's the key to vivid descriptive writing: creating memorable images.

Here is another example of pictorial writing: this time a specific place is being described.

> Just before sundown in the latter part of an August day, an unexpected *summer fog nudged* in from the Atlantic Ocean. The *damp cloud enveloped* the Brooklyn Bridge, swept across New York City, and *blanketed* the entire Bronx area. For a whole night the white counterpane *drooped silently* over the *misty harbor* waters and it appeared that time stood still.

To write descriptively, you must envision what you want the reader to see, and the best way to capture a person, place, or thing is to see it first in your own mind's eye. The process that enables you to create images is not so mysterious. Before you begin to write, close your eyes and get a vivid snapshot of the object you want to "portrait" through your writing. Ask yourself what you see, hear, feel, smell, touch, taste. When you make the scene come alive in your mind's eye, you will be better able to make it come alive for your reader as well. To awaken your "writing senses" use the following lists to assist you.

Sight Words	Sound Words	Taste Words	Touch Words	Smell Words
freckled	crash	buttery	leathery	moldy
shabby	hubbub	salty	cool	fragrant
iridescent	hum	spicy	fuzzy	dank
elegant	shuffle	sour	lukewarm	piney
hysterical	musical	bitter	sticky	aromatic
crooked	giggle	creamy	sharp	earthy
rotted	thunder	unripe	wooly	balmy
opaque	explode	sweet	smooth	stagnant
bruised	murmur	burnt	steamy	pungent
slender	snap	spoiled	dry	smoky
muscular	bedlam	peppery	cold	fishy
hollow	screech	bland	lumpy	rancid
mahogany	whistle	crisp	sandy	fresh

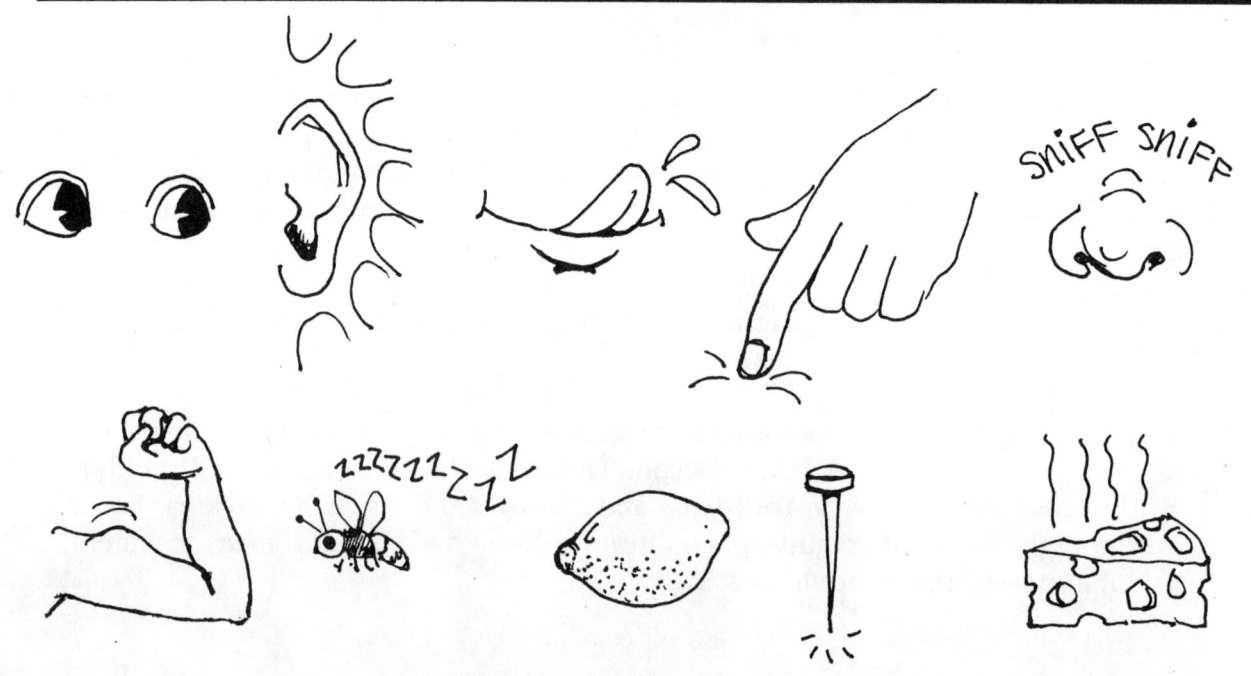

Descriptive Writing "Lingo"

Another way to write descriptively is to learn well the language of the topic you will be describing. That language is often referred to as lingo. *Lingo* is slang for *language* and every subject has its own specialized language. Writing about a specific subject demands that you know its language in order to write well about it. One good way to learn the language of any subject is to look at the way professionals write on the topic. In order to see how professionals handle a subject, just get newspaper articles, magazine articles, or books on the topic. As you read from the material, notice the specialized lingo the writer uses. You can model the writer's word choices to enhance your writing.

Imagine that you have to write a descriptive paragraph for an English assignment and you want to write about the upcoming Super Bowl championship game. First, get copies of newspapers or magazine articles dealing with the game. Then read the materials, and make a list of football terms (verbs, adjectives, and/or nouns) from the sources to help you make your writing on the topic more descriptive, more lively, more professional. Your list of borrowed words or phrases might include the following: four rookie runners, total interceptions, late-scoring drive, home-team advantage, physical offense, solid passing game, the take-away battle won the game, the snap was high, roughing the quarterback, etc.

Perhaps you would rather write your assignment about a rock concert. Then your lingo list might be first performance, within rock circles, greatest soloist in rock, easy to record, among instrumentalists, listeners found the concert totally rhythmic, *Billboard's* number one group, distinctive sound, etc. Just keep in mind, that whatever topic you are writing on, if you use the lingo of a subject like a pro, you will greatly enliven your writing and you will be better able to hold your reader's attention.

The fictitious paragraph which follows could have been written by a newspaper sportswriter around the time when a Super Bowl showdown was about to begin. The italicized words are terms you could use for a Descriptive Writing Lingo List about the game.

Showdown on the Road to Super Bowl XXXIV

Source: *USA SPORTS.*   January 17, 1999

Author: Alex Smithe

Last weekend, the *Redskins systematically tore apart* the *Lions* 41-10 and *meet* the *Bills*, 11-6 *winners* against *Denver*, in the *AFC title game* in *Super Bowl* XXXIV. Washington (17-1) and *Buffalo* (16-2) had the *best records* in their *conferences*, setting up the Super Bowl most *fans* and experts anticipated. *Art Monk*, the Washington Redskins' quiet-man's *wide-receiver* and *first-round pick*, summed up his feelings on the hoopla saying, "It's everything that I don't particularly care for, all the media attention; it's a lot of confusion." But when asked to sum up what might happen in the game, Monk said, "I can see a *punt being blocked*, an *interception before halftime*, but I know we are committed to one another and will do everything possible to see that we not only do our job, but that everybody else stays on track and does his job too." But his *team* is counting on him to get the job done. For once, Monk is healthy after a *regular season* where he *caught 71 passes* for *1048 yards, fourteen TDs*. In the *playoff games*, he had eight catches for 159 yards and a TD. The Redskins have high hopes that their *all-star team* can deliver the goods on Sunday in the Minneapolis *Metrodome*.

Now It's Your Turn

My Descriptive Writing Lingo

My source is _____.

The author (if given) is _____.

My descriptive writing topic is _____.

1. _____	2. _____
3. _____	4. _____
5. _____	6. _____
7. _____	8. _____
9. _____	10. _____
11. _____	12. _____
13. _____	14. _____
15. _____	16. _____
17. _____	18. _____
19. _____	20. _____

Now It's Your Turn

Descriptive Writing

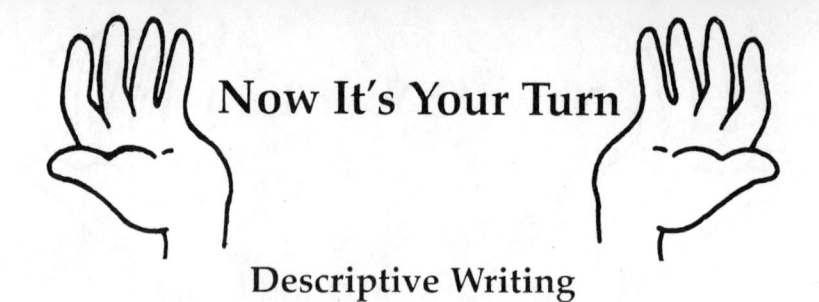

Put your five senses to work for you. Write a descriptive account of a favorite person, place, or thing in your life. Remember, first close your eyes and "picture" what you will write about. Get a vivid image before you start to write. Your writing will become "real"; then it will become authentic; then it will be truly descriptive.

Now It's Your Turn

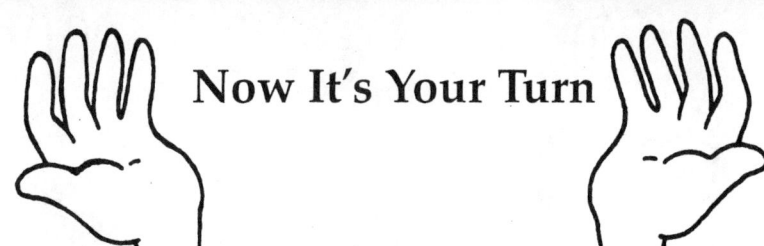

Descriptive Writing

Now It's Your Turn

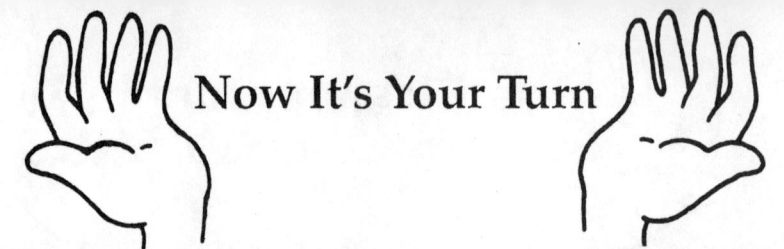

Descriptive Writing (cont'd.)

Expository Writing

Expository writing is writing that shows, explains, or informs. It is the writing you read in your schoolbooks, the writing you read when you are following steps to make a recipe, or the writing you read when you are putting together a new bike. So, when you write an expository paragraph or essay, you must make it eminently clear what you want the reader to know or to do. As the writer, you must assume that your reader knows nothing about your topic, and you must write so precisely that anyone who reads what you have written will understand it. For example, if a friend is absent from math class and the teacher asks you to explain the lesson to your friend, your explanation must be clear, accurate, and well-organized, so that your friend will be able to understand the lesson he or she missed.

Writing an expository piece appears to be a simple task, but it is not. However, there are some writers' tricks that you can use to help you succeed at the task. First, sit down and carefully think through and plan what you need to write; in other words, organize your thoughts. For example, if you are writing a recipe about how to make a salad, you will need to arrange the steps so that the reader will be able to follow your instructions. Then, you will need to use specific terms such as *tear*, *peel*, *slice*, or *chop* to assist the reader's understanding of specifically what is to be done.

However, if you are giving a set of instructions to a new student on how to get to the gym from your science classroom, your explanation might include terminology such as "Turn left at the end of the English wing, go past the main office, and head down the white-tiled ramp, leading to the double wooden doors to the cork gym. You can't miss it."

Test to see if your expository piece can be clearly understood by getting someone to make or do just what you describe. Keep in mind that one of the most important ingredients in writing an expository piece is to organize it logically, sequentially, or chronologically. Then the task should be easy for any reader to accomplish.

spread jelly on the bread.

Read the paragraph that follows and notice the way in which the directions are designed to help someone who doesn't know how to get to O'Hare International Airport.

> The fastest way to O'Hare Airport from here is to take the expressway. *Go three blocks north* to Route 59. *Turn left,* and *go three miles west.* Then you will notice a sign marked, "To Chicago." Turn right. On the expressway, you will *travel due east for about a mile* when you will see another sign saying, O'Hare *next right."* Be ready to turn. Once you make the right turn, the airport will be practically *in front of you.* Follow the signs, and you can't miss it.

Notice how the italicized words tell the reader exactly what he or she needs to do to get to O'Hare Airport.

Another kind of expository writing compares or contrasts two different topics. For example, you might be asked to compare and contrast two historic figures like Benjamin Franklin and Thomas Jefferson, or to compare and contrast two different books like *The Incredible Journey* and *Rascal.* This kind of assignment is best handled by making lists showing how the subjects are alike and different. Once you have created these lists, you will be better prepared to write a paragraph, essay, or theme explaining the similarities and/or differences of the two topics. Use the following example as a guide.

Thomas Jefferson   **Benjamin Franklin**

Alike

- Born and raised in the 1700s
- Signed the Declaration of Independence
- Sided with the Colonists against King George III
- Served as ambassador to France

Thomas Jefferson	Benjamin Franklin

Different

• Attended the best schools, tutored • President of Univ. of Virginia • Third U.S. President	• Attended school for two years, apprenticed • Experimented with electricity • Postmaster General

Incredible Journey	Rascal

Alike

• Animal story
• Lively characters
• Rural setting
• Children involved in story

Incredible Journey	Rascal

Different

• Setting: Ontario • Time: 1950s • Animals make way home	• Setting: Wisconsin • Time: 1940s • Rascal must leave home

Copyright © 1994, Good Apple

GA1491

Now It's Your Turn

My Expository Writing

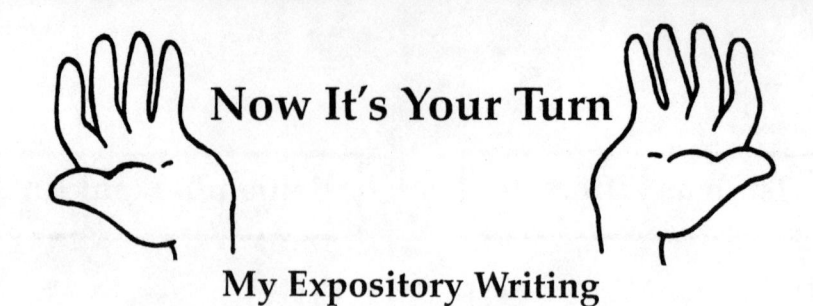

1. Pick one of the following topics on which to write an expository paragraph.

    - How to clean your room
    - How to brush your teeth
    - How to make spaghetti
    - How to organize a baseball card collection
    - Your choice of topic

Now It's Your Turn

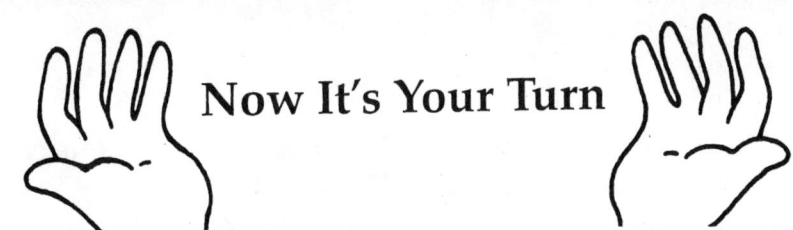

Expository Writing

2. Try your hand at comparing and contrasting two topics of your choice, using the models given in this activity to help you. Then use the next page to write a comparison/contrasting theme.

Alike

Different

Now It's Your Turn

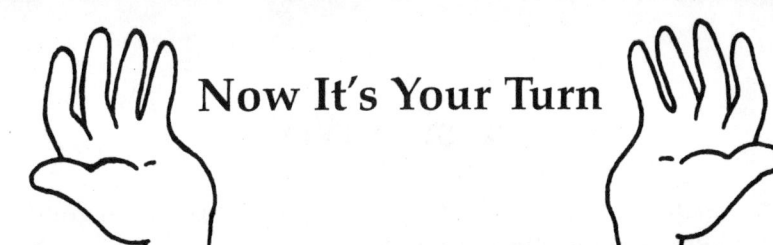

Expository Writing: Comparing and Contrasting

Persuasive Writing

Persuasive writing is quite easy to do because it is a form of something that you do each and every day. *Persuasion* is the art of *getting people to do what you want them to do* ("Come uptown with me after school."), or getting something you want from someone ("Mom, I just have to have a new stereo; everyone else is getting one."), or getting others to agree to your opinion ("I think school should be cancelled once and for all.") on some topic of importance.

You are surrounded by the media–newspapers, magazines, radio, and television–which are all trying to persuade you to subscribe, to listen to their station or channel, or to buy their advertised products. Wall Street executives pay thousands of dollars to advertising agencies to come up with "catchy" words, phrases, or tunes in order to get you to spend your hard-earned dollars on their goods or services. Look around you. Notice how many people are wearing the same brand of clothes, the same style of shoes, the same kind of jewelry. Why? Because some clever ad agents have convinced you and your friends that you "need" the clothes, the shoes, or the jewelry in order for you to be in fashion, or in order for you to be in with the right crowd. This technique is known as the art of persuasion. Once you learn the basic formula for persuading, you will be able to apply the persuasive process to oral reports, written themes, and/or lively debates. All you need to do is follow these steps.

1. Choose a topic you care about.
   - endangered species
   - peer pressure
   - freedom of speech

2. Start by stating your opinion.
   - I think taking care of the earth's animals is everyone's responsibility.
   - Resisting peer pressure is very difficult.
   - Freedom of speech is a precious right most Americans take for granted.

3. Uphold your opinion with at least three supporting details.

4. End your presentation with a brief summary which restates your opinion and which leaves your audience convinced that your opinion is the best.

A Sample Persuasive Paragraph:

Homework should be outlawed. Wait. Before you walk away or cheer, let me explain. I mean homework that's brainless. Busywork teachers give students to do which takes no thought, effort, or real learning should be abolished. For example, why should I do fifty similar math problems when I can prove I know how to do that particular math assignment by doing five or ten of these problems? Or, why should I write my spelling words twenty-five times each, when I might misspell the word at the beginning, and then I'll write it incorrectly twenty-five times. And, furthermore, why would a teacher teach students to learn about poetic rhyme and rhythm by asking them to "drum out" the beat of three sonnets while saying the poems out loud at home? Surely the poems weren't written to be "drummed out on a desk." Don't you agree that these are examples of homework, busywork? So, if teachers aren't going to give meaningful, interesting and stimulating homework, students should revolt and ask for some!

WHAT? YOU GOTTA' BE KIDDING!

I'M STILL NOT CONVINCED, but TELL ME MORE.

OKAY, I HATE to ADMIT IT, but YOU HAVE A POINT.

Notice how the paragraph begins with a strong opinion (homework–outlawed), is followed by three strong supporting details (a ton of math problems, rote writing of spelling words, and a senseless exploration of the stressed and unstressed syllables in poems), and concludes with the irresistible imploring remark, "Don't you agree . . . ?" What overworked student, caring teacher, and thinking parent could possibly not see the logic of this argument against "brainless homework"?

A good way to find a topic that will appeal to you for a persuasive piece of writing is to look on the editorial pages of a newspaper. They are filled with people's opinions, and you will often find opposing opinions on the same topic on the same page or pages. Once you have found a topic that appeals to you, cut out the article and examine it to see how it is written and then use it as a model for your own persuasive argument on the same theme.

A very powerful form of persuasion is *propaganda*. It is a technique used to sway people's thinking. Propaganda is used on TV ads to get you to go see the latest movie, buy the newest product, or vote for a certain political candidate. Not all propaganda is false, nor is all propaganda true. So you need to be able to distinguish between what is fact and what is fiction in what you see, what you hear, and what you read. Here are some points to look for when you are reading, watching, or listening to media.

- **loaded words**–used to appeal to your emotions, not your reasoning skills. This propaganda technique appeals to people's hopes and fears. Look for loaded words such as *unwanted, dull, health, vitality, patriotic duty*. For example, "Is unwanted soap leaving a dull, dirty film on your hair? Then give your hair the look of health and vitality by using Sparkle Shampoo."

- **bandwagon technique**–used to convince you that if you don't act immediately, you'll feel left out. An example is "Eight out of ten teenagers have switched to new neon-colored watchbands. Join the fun; get yours today."

- **testimonial**–uses a famous person to recommend that you buy, do, or believe in something (a cause) or someone (a politician). "Bill Brothers, our U.S. Olympic downhill gold medal winner starts every day with a bowl of Chocolate Corn Crunchies. Why not start your day with Crunchies?"

- **faulty cause and effect**–implies that one factor has a positive impact on another factor. "We've been at this location for thirty years. We are the best business in Towndown."

Now It's Your Turn

Propaganda—the Art of Persuasion

1. Write a sentence or two that use loaded words.

2. Create an ad that calls for people to jump on the "bandwagon."

3. Use someone famous to recommend others buy, do, or believe as he or she does.

4. Design a slogan that uses the cause and effect propaganda technique.

Now It's Your Turn

1. Select a topic that appeals to you or one which you care a great deal about. Write the topic in a persuasive mode on the lines provided.

   _____

   _____

2. Read about the topic in a variety of sources–magazines, encyclopedias, newspapers, or almanacs–and jot down at least three important points to support your persuasive theme or argument.

   a. _____

   _____

   b. _____

   _____

   c. _____

   _____

3. Write a strong concluding paragraph for your piece of persuasive writing. Then on the next page put your persuasive theme together.

   _____

   _____

   _____

   _____

   _____

   _____

   _____

   _____

   _____

Now It's Your Turn

My Persuasive Writing

Journals and Diaries

Journals were made famous and popular in America in 1814 with the publication of *The Journal of Meriwether Lewis and William Clark*. In 1804 our third President, Thomas Jefferson, said to Lewis, "I am going to send an expedition to explore the West and you will lead it," and Meriwether chose his friend William Clark to lead the expedition with him. On the rainy Monday morning of May 14, 1804, the group of explorers climbed into boats and pushed off to chart the region acquired from France by President Jefferson in 1803 under the terms of the agreement that came to be called the Louisiana Purchase.

The purpose of the mission was to chart the vast territory that stretched from the Mississippi River to the Pacific Ocean and the great Northwest. Over the next two and a half years the team forged through rivers, journeyed over plains, squeezed through mountain passes, and endured troublesome weather and harsh living conditions in order to scientifically document this vast wilderness for President Jefferson, for the country, for its citizens.

Lewis and Clark recorded what they saw (plant and animal life), where they went (geographical regions), the weather, and the people they met (numerous Indian tribes) along the length of the route. They made maps, kept charts, and logged in journals all that they saw, encountered, and experienced. These journals became invaluable to President Jefferson, his Cabinet, and to all Americans. In fact, the journals are still read today by students, history buffs, scientists, and naturalists. The journals are well-written and lushly illustrated, and they remain as significant in the twentieth century as they were when they were first written in the nineteenth century.

Diaries, on the other hand, are for your eyes only. They should be written to keep the events of your life recorded on a daily basis. In fact, diaries have a place to enter the date and traditionally begin, "Dear Diary, today. . . ." Diaries serve as a means for you to write your secrets, hopes, and dreams for a silent audience; and they are often kept private and secure by an outside lock to which you alone hold the key.

Sometimes when a famous person dies, his or her diary is made public so others may get a better understanding of the deceased, and so that the famous person's thoughts and feelings can be revealed in order that those left behind have a clearer insight into the actions of that person. *The Diary of Anne Frank* is such a document. Anne's vivid account recounts the pain and hope she and her family experienced while they were forced to hide in a secret attic in an Amsterdam office building during the Nazi occupation of the Netherlands. Anne's two-year diary was found after she was sent to the Nazi concentration camp at Belsen. It has become a poignant legacy for all young people. Anne's diary was published in 1947 and is still read with keen interest by junior high and high school students today. It has even been made into a play.

Perhaps some day the journal and/or diary that you are keeping will become as famous as Lewis and Clark's or Anne Frank's. But both kinds of writing are valuable for future generations as you record your experiences, dreams, your opinions, beliefs, and daily events. Make journal or diary writing a habit. Set aside some time each day to jot down the things as they happen, while they are fresh, before they are forgotten.

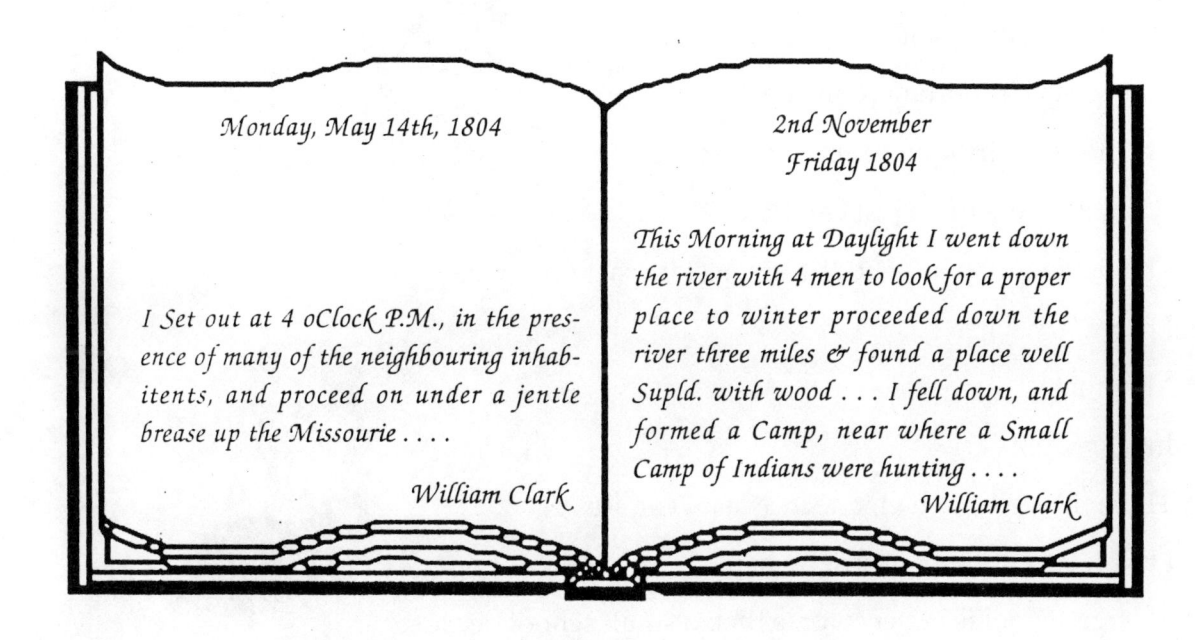

Monday, May 14th, 1804

I Set out at 4 oClock P.M., in the presence of many of the neighbouring inhabitents, and proceed on under a jentle brease up the Missourie . . . .

William Clark

2nd November
Friday 1804

This Morning at Daylight I went down the river with 4 men to look for a proper place to winter proceeded down the river three miles & found a place well Supld. with wood . . . I fell down, and formed a Camp, near where a Small Camp of Indians were hunting . . . .

William Clark

Journal Writing

Here are some topics you might like to write about in your journal. Remember a journal should be used to explore, experiment, and examine a variety of writing genre (poems, fiction, nonfiction) and topics. You can write whatever you like, just so you write something every day. You might describe a teacher, a friend, a class, a favorite activity, a movie, or a video. Just write something. It is one of the best habits you can acquire.

Suggested Journal Writing Topics

- I was most happy when . . .
- In my leisure time I like to . . .
- A time when I wanted something very badly and my parents wouldn't let me get it was . . .
- Something I am very proud of is . . .
- Loyalty is important in a friendship because . . .
- Freedom is important to me because . . .
- The neatest birthday I ever had was . . .
- A habit I have that I just can't break is . . .
- The person who has had the greatest impact on my life is . . .
- I get angry when . . .
- My greatest strength is . . .
- In a group, I . . .
- Three things I've changed since last year are . . .
- I think parents are too strict when . . .
- A large school is better/worse than a small school because . . .
- My hero is . . .
- Things I'm best at are . . .
- I feel tests are . . .
- The funniest TV program is . . .
- The best book I ever read is . . .
- Responsibility to me means . . .
- What I like about my family is . . .
- Being informed about global events is . . .

Now It's Your Turn

My Journal Writing

Now It's Your Turn

_____
Today's date

Dear Diary,

_____
_____
_____
_____
_____
_____
_____

_____
Today's date

Dear Diary,

_____
_____
_____
_____
_____
_____
_____

Writing Letters and Thank-You Notes

There is no doubt in anyone's mind that we live in an electronic age surrounded by audiocassettes, videocassettes, compact disks (CDs), laser disks, and FAX machines; but the art and necessity of writing letters and thank-you notes is not dead. For example, if you buy a pair of gym shoes and they fall apart in six weeks' time (and this is not the result of abuse on your part), and you did not save the register receipt when you purchased your shoes, the best way to try to get your shoes replaced is to write a letter to the manufacturer. You state exactly why your shoes fell apart and what you would like the company to do to stand behind their product. If your letter is written well, you could get the company to replace your shoes at little or no cost to you. Read the sample letter which follows to learn about the main parts of a letter and to see how to construct a compelling letter.

Block Form Letter
Return address

800 E. Main Street
Barrington, IL 60010
March 15, 1999

James
    Jack
        Jones

Inside address (to whom you are sending the letter)

Ms. New Shoe
Customer Service Representative
Great New Shoe Company
50 W. Great New Shoe Drive
Chicago, IL 60611

Salutation

Dear Ms. Shoe:

Body of the letter

On January 31, 1999, I purchased a pair of size 6 jogging Great New Shoes at The We Have It All Store, in my neighborhood. I really like the shoes, but the soles have come loose, the tongue has fallen off, and the awesome neon colors have faded. It appears that my pair of shoes is a "lemon." I have purchased shoes from your company before, and I have never had these kinds of problems. I know you stand behind your products, so I want to send you my pair of "lemons" if you are willing to send me a new pair of shoes to replace them. Unfortunately, I no longer have the receipt for the shoes, but your research department can verify that I have not had my Great New Shoes for more than six weeks.

I look forward to hearing from you. I know you represent a good company, Ms. Shoe, and I know your company will stand behind their product. Thank you for your consideration of my problem.

Closing

Sincerely,

Signature

James Jack Jones

You will be amazed with the results this kind of letter will get you. If you call the company, they will listen to your complaint, but may not be as willing to do anything about it as they would be if you sent them a letter. It is still true today that, "actions (writing a letter) speak louder than words (a phone call)."

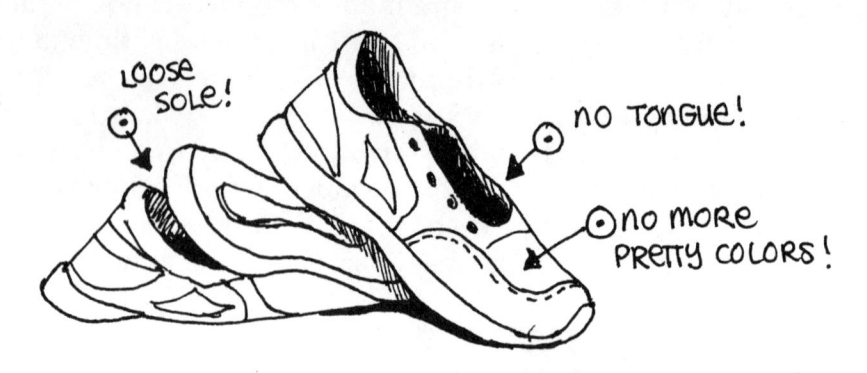

Like letters to companies requesting action on their part, thank-you notes have a way of getting action from their receivers. If you have just gotten your most longed-for birthday gift from your grandparents, a thank-you note telling them how much you like the present they have sent you will be treasured by them and make them more willing to send you another gift the next time your birthday rolls around. After all, grandparents can proudly hang your thank-you note on the refrigerator, but they can't hang your phone message on the refrigerator. A sample thank-you note follows.

Inside address	514 Miller Rd. Chicago, IL 60633 March 17, 1999	**Thank You**
Greeting	Dear Grandma and Grandpa,	
Body	I just want to thank you so much for the awesome, new CDs you sent for my birthday. I just love listening to them. I think the plastic case cover featuring the group is so sweet. I can't thank you enough, because I've been dying to add these CDs to my ever-growing collection. You are the greatest grandparents in the whole world. I can't wait till you come to visit; then we can listen to my new CDs together. Thanks again. I love both of you.	
Closing	Hugs and kisses,	**Judy**
Signature	Judy	**Jane** **Jones**

Now It's Your Turn

1. Write a block form letter to any company making a request.

Inside address

Salutation

Body

Closing

Signature

Now It's Your Turn

2. Write a block form thank-you note.

Inside address

Greeting

Body

Closing

Signature

How to Address an Envelope

Envelope: Business Form

James Jack Jones
800 E. Main St.
Barrington, IL 60010

          Ms. New Shoe
          Customer Service Representative
          Great New Shoe Company
          50 W. Great New Shoe Drive
          Chicago, IL 60611

Envelope: Friendly Form

Judy Jane Jones
514 Miller Rd.
Chicago, IL 60633

          Mr. and Mrs. J. Jones
          514 W. State St.
          Chicago, IL 60611

Now It's Your Turn

Prepare an envelope for your business letter and your thank-you note.

Envelope: Business Form

Envelope: Friendly Form

How to Fold a Letter

Folding a business letter properly is important. The format for correct folding is as follows. Start at the bottom of the paper and fold it one-third of the way towards the top. Next, take the folded one-third section and fold it over so that the top of the paper is no longer visible. When properly folded, the letter should be one-third its original size, and it should fit neatly into an envelope. When placing the letter in an envelope, put it in so that when the receiver opens the letter, he or she will be greeted with your salutation of "Dear Sir," "Dear Ms.," etc.

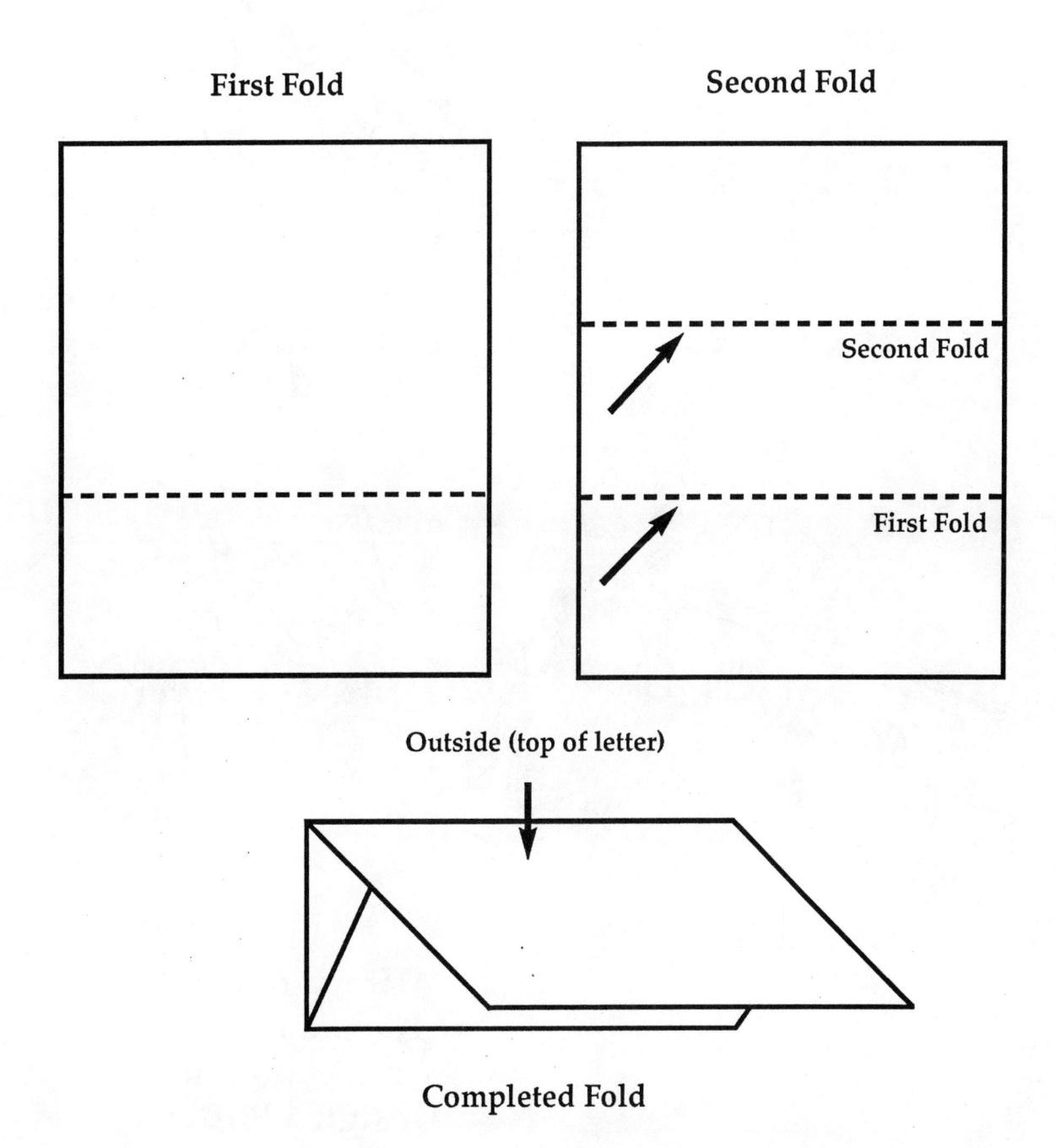

First Fold

Second Fold

Second Fold

First Fold

Outside (top of letter)

Completed Fold

Getting Published

Enter Contests **Illustrate Your Ideas**

Write a Journal,
Keep a Diary,
Create a Book,
Design a Poster

Getting Published

As a writer there is nothing more exhilarating than seeing your name in print. It is like the winning run of the writer's baseball game; it is like the final basket before the buzzer of a basketball game. You are already a "published" author if you have written thank-you notes for birthday presents, if you have written a letter to a company requesting a sample product, or if you submitted a story to the school newspaper and it was published. In fact, all students are "published" when they let others see their writing, when their writing is posted on a bulletin board, or when their parents read their writing. Seeing your name in print gives you a feeling of power, and sharing ideas gives you a real sense of the importance of writing. Publishing gives you an audience, gives you an "ear" for your "music," gives you reasons to write.

You can become published in a more formal sense in a variety of ways. First, you can publish your own writing in a spiral-bound notebook in which you fill the pages with poems, stories, memoirs, sports statistics, daily happenings, thoughts, reactions, or whatever. Writing on a daily basis gets you in a writing habit.

Another way to become formally published is to join the school newspaper or yearbook staff, or a writing club for which you can write feature articles, draw cartoons, create illustrations, produce captions, or serve as a staff member in order to share your writing.

A third way to be formally published is to send your writing to commercial publishers. There are many publications which publish student writing on a regular basis. A list of these publishers appears at the end of this activity. Finally, you could enter writing contests. Many preteen and teen magazines feature contests for young writers. Read and follow the rules carefully, send off your manuscript, and good luck. Just keep in mind, if you don't write, you can't get published. Like the batter at the plate with a chance to win the game, you've got to swing at the ball if you hope to hit a homer. You must write, if you hope to get formally published.

IT'S A HIT!

Publishers of Student Writings

The following list represents some of the publishers of student writing. Before you submit any pieces of writing, however, it is a good idea to send for the publisher's submission guidelines and pay a small fee for a sample issue of their magazine, newsletter or the like, to assure that you are sending the kind of writing published by the company. Another good idea is to check the publisher's magazines out of the public library and read several issues to get a "flavor" for the kind of writing the publisher is looking for. Be sure you submit to the publisher the kind of writing he or she publishes. There is no sense in sending your poems to a publisher who doesn't publish poetry. Next, have a friend or parent proofread your work before you submit it so that you are sending off your best, error-free work. Check out a book at the library that shows you how to write a query letter and cover letter. And, finally, if you see *SASE*, it means send a **s**elf-**a**ddressed **s**tamped **e**nvelope to assure that your manuscript will be returned to you.

All American High School Magazine. Box 254800, Sacramento, CA 95865. Accepts fiction.

American Girl. Girl Scouts of the USA, 800 Third Ave., New York, NY 10022. Stories, poetry, art, puzzles, and craft projects. Girls 6-11.

American Newspaper Carrier. Box 15300, Winston-Salem, NC 27113. Light fiction, 1800-2000 words. Mystery, adventure, inspirational, editorials. Ages 14-17.

The Beehive. 201 Eighth Ave. South, Nashville, TN 37203. Stories. 4th to 6th graders. 700 words or less.

Boys' Life. 1325 Walnut Hill Lane, Irving, TX 75038-3096. Wants interesting ideas for column on hobbies.

Bread. 6401 The Paseo, Kansas City, MO 64131. Religious and nonreligious articles 500 to 1200 words, fiction to 1500 words, poetry to 20 lines. Teenagers.

Canadian Children's Magazine. 4150 Bracken Avenue, Victoria, B.C., Canada V8X 3N8. Poetry, fillers, puzzles, educational articles to 1000 words and fiction to 1500 words. Elementary school children.

Creative Kids P.O. Box 6448, Mobile, AL 36660. Poetry, short stories, plays, magazines, music, games, activities, limericks, parodies, prose, cartoons, artwork, photography, reviews of books and games, pen pals, and computer programs. Ages 5-15.

Child Life. 1100 Waterway Blvd., P.O. Box 567B, Indianapolis, IN 46206. Science fiction and mystery magazine for children. Letters, poems, art, and short stories with a science fiction or mystery theme. Ages 7-11.

Children's Playmate. 100 Waterway Blvd., P.O. Box 567, Indianapolis, IN 46206. Poetry, jokes, riddles, art, and stories for ages 3-8.

Cricket. P.O. Box 300, Peru, IL 61354. Literary magazine for ages 5-12. Letters, riddles, and a monthly contest for stories, poetry, and art.

Ebony, Jr. 820 South Michigan Ave., Chicago, IL 60605. For all children but slanted towards black children. Letters, stories, poetry, jokes, riddles. Ages 6-12.

Gifted Children Monthly. "Spinoff Editor," P.O. Box 115, Sewell, NJ 08080. Jokes, riddles, mazes, artwork, puzzles, short stories, poetry.

Highlights for Children. Box 269, Columbus, OH 43272-0002. For ages 2-12. Poetry, stories, letters, jokes, riddles, and black and white artwork.

Teenage. 1650 Zanker Rd., No. 222, San Jose, CA 95112. Fiction, nonfiction, and fillers. High school.

Jack and Jill. 1100 Waterway Blvd., P.O. Box 567, Indianapolis, IN 46206. Letters, poems, art, photos of children and short stories. Ages 5-12.

Just About Me. Ensio Industries, 247 Marlee Ave., Suite 206, Toronto, Ontario, Canada M6B 4B8. Fiction and poetry for girls 12-19.

Prism (A Magazine by and for Gifted and Talented). 2455 E. Sunrise Blvd., Ste. 300, Ft. Lauderdale, FL 33304. Poetry, short stories, riddles, mazes, artwork, puzzles, pen pals, interviews, comic strips, news of children's achievements, descriptions of craft projects and activities, and letters to the editor. Ages 10-18.

Purple Cow. 3423 Piedmont Rd. NE, Ste. 320, Atlanta, GA 30305-1742. Fiction and fillers. Ages 12-18.

Ranger Rick. 1412 16th Street NW, Washington, DC 20036. Fiction, nonfiction, puzzles on nature/ecology themes.

Read Magazine. c/o Field Publications, 245 Long Hill Rd., Middletown, CT 06457. Mazes, artwork, puzzles, short stories, poetry, and nonfiction. Ages 11-14.

Scholastic Scope. 730 Broadway, New York, NY 10003. Poetry, stories, plays, and mini mysteries. Grades 7-12.

Scholastic Voice. 730 Broadway, New York, NY 10003. Poetry and stories less than 500 words. Grades 7-13.

Seventeen. 850 Third Ave., New York, NY 10022. Short fiction, poetry, mood pieces, opinion columns, personal experiences. Girls 12-18.

Stone Soup. P.O. Box 83, Santa Cruz, CA 95063. Free verse poetry, short stories, artwork, book reviews. Ages 8-13.

The Sunshine News. Canada Sunshine Publishing, Ltd., 465 King Street East #14A, Toronto, Ontario, Canada M5A 1L6. High school.

Wee Wisdom. Unity Village, MO 64065. Poetry and short stories of 100 words or less. All ages.

Weewish Tree. American Indian Historical Society, 1451 Masonic Ave., San Francisco, CA 94117. Poetry, stories, art with Indian-related themes. All ages.

T.Q. (Teen Quest) Good News Broadcasting Association, Inc., Box 82808, Lincoln, NE 68501. Short filler. Ages 12-16.

Young World. 1100 Waterway Blvd., P.O. Box 567, Indianapolis, IN 46206. Letters, poetry, art, jokes, short stories, and articles. Ages 10-14.

Writing Contests to Enter

Elias Liberman Student Poetry Award. Poetry Society of America, Gramercy Park, New York, NY 10003. High school juniors and seniors.

Guideposts Magazine Youth Writing Contest. Guideposts Associate Inc., 5999 Stevenson Avenue, Alexandria, VA 22304. High school juniors and seniors.

National Achievement in Writing Awards. National Council of Teachers of English, 1111 Kenyon Road, Urbana, IL 61801. Essay writing. Senior high school students.

Cricket. Box 300, Peru, IL 61354. Story-writing contests. Ages 13 and under.

Young Writer's Contest Foundation. P.O. Box 6092, McLean, VA 22106, 1st-8th grades. Yearly contest, deadline usually at the end of November.

Often local writing groups and public libraries host writing contests for students. Check your local newspaper for details. Whether you write for yourself or a large or small audience (classmates, relatives, contests), daily writing should be your goal, and you must keep in mind that writing, like any other "sport," improves with practice, daily workouts, good coaching, participating with others who enjoy the "sport," and the self-discipline that encourages players to play and writers to write.

Note: Every effort has been made, at the time of this publication, to insure the accuracy of the information included in this book. We cannot guarantee, however, that the agencies and organizations we have mentioned will continue to operate or to maintain these current locations indefinitely.

Now It's Your Turn

My Plans to Get Published

1. Three things I like to write about are

   _____
   _____
   _____

2. Three ways I plan to publish are

   _____
   _____
   _____

3. Three contests I plan to enter are

   _____
   _____
   _____

Make, Take, Invigorate

Book Reports　　　　　　　　Book Reports

Banners　　　　　　　　　　Banners

Collages　　　　　　　　　　Collages

Posters　　　　　　　　　　Posters

Mobiles　　　　　　　　　　Mobiles

Shoe Box Floats　　　　　　Shoe Box Floats

Save the Panda . . . Save the Earth.

Book Report Ideas
Forty-Five Ways to Give 'em

1. Make a filmstrip on a long sheet of white paper with different pictures on it. Cut a slit at the top and bottom of a shoe box, and show the filmstrip on the machine made from a cardboard box by pulling the paper slowly through the box.

2. Create a poster depicting your favorite character or scene from the book. Be sure to put the title and author's name on the poster (see "How to Make a Poster" on page 104).

3. Design a shadow box by putting colorful figures and background scenery in the box and use the figures to tell about the book.

4. Cut pictures out of magazines and make a collage of a main event or main character in the book.

5. Do a dramatic reading of your favorite part of the book.

6. Draw a large illustration of the main character and give a thorough description of the character. For example, What does he or she look like? How would you describe his or her personality (loving, kind, curious, mischievous, determined, lazy, shy, etc.)? Find two or three examples from the book showing what the character said or did to help the audience learn about the main character.

7. Create your own book jacket. Not only design the cover of the jacket, but also write the blurb for the book's front and back flaps. Include a brief description of the story's background, where and when the story takes place, and describe the most exciting incidents that take place in the story. Finally, give some information about the author.

8. Write a simpler version of the book to present to younger children. You might want to put your version in a "big book" format.

9. Dress up the way one of the characters of the story would be dressed and tell the story.

10. Alone, or with others, act out one of the major scenes in the book.

11. Use the friendly letter style and write to the book's author. Send your letter to the publisher and they will forward your letter to the author.

12. Imagine that you have been hired by a local TV station to interview the author of a book. Make a list of questions you would want to ask the author. For example, you might want to know where the idea for the book came from, if the main character is based on someone the author knows, why the author selected the theme for the book, etc. After you have planned your questions, write out the answers you think the author might give you, and let someone else take the role of the author for your interview. You could make an audio or visual presentation of your author-interview.

13. Get a friend to stage a debate of the merits of a book. Each of you must take opposite sides—one will like the book, the other should dislike it. Focus the debate on specific points on which you differ (I like the plot/I don't like the plot, or I think there was a lot of action in the book/I didn't think there was enough action in the book, the characters were believable/the characters were unbelievable). Each should use passages from the book to support your point of view.

14. Assume the role of the main character of the book. Give a first-person account of your role. Add authenticity to your role by dressing the part. Then tell about the problems the main character faced and how he or she overcame them. Next, introduce one or two other characters and explain how the main character interacted with them in the story.

15. Create an ad for the book that might appear in a magazine or on TV. Keep in mind that ads are short on words, focused on the visual, and designed to get others to want to read the book.

16. Pretend that you have been hired by the local newspaper to write a book review for students your age. Write a review of the book by briefly outlining the plot, introducing the characters, and giving your "professional" opinion about the book.

17. Create a crossword puzzle for the book. Others who have read the book might like to try their hand at completing the crossword puzzle.

18. When you go to the movies or rent a video, you often get a sneak preview of coming attractions. Put together a sneak preview of your book for the class. Give them enough information to whet their appetites so that they will want to read the book.

19. Try the opposite of a sneak preview. Prepare a cliff-hanger by providing your audience with some background about the plot, setting, and characters. Then read the most exciting passage, but don't read what finally happens. End by commenting, "Now if you would like to know how the book ends, read (name of the book) to find out."

20. Make believe that you are an editor for a major publishing company whose job it is to select books for your company to publish. Sit around the table with other members of the company and debate with the selection committee why you wanted the book (you have read) published.

21. Write a letter to a pen pal outlining why he or she should read the book.

22. Make a list of five traits that you admired about one of the characters. Then read a passage for each trait from the text to show what makes you admire this character.

23. Change the time (past, present, or future) in which the book takes place. Read an exciting passage from the book which demonstrates the actual time of the book, and then read the same passage as it would be written with the time changed.

24. Use any style to write a poem about the book. Include clues to the plot, setting, and characters.

25. Write about the funniest, saddest, scariest, etc., part of the book.

26. Make a mural depicting the most interesting parts of the book.

27. Find out more about the author and write a short biography of him or her.

28. Write a sequel to the book.

29. Make pipe cleaner, wire figures, or hand puppets and put on a "show" about the book.

30. Write a new ending to the story.

31. Write a quiz to give to others who have already read the book.

32. Draw a picture of one or more characters or scenes from the book.

33. Pretend you are a famous Hollywood director. Select a favorite scene in the book and write it as a movie, video, or TV script (like a play), explaining the set and props as well as the conversation or dialogue.

34. Make a mobile telling about the characters and/or plot of the story. (See pages 108-111.)

35. Out of clay, wood, or papier-mâché make three or more models of the setting, important events, or characters.

36. Novels are about conflict. Make a video depicting the major conflict in the book.

37. Write a five-to-ten-day diary for the leading character in the book.

38. Make a chart to compare your way of life to that of the main character. Show how you are different and what you have in common. Your comparison might include where you live (urban vs. rural setting), facts about your families, interests, personalities, goals, etc.

39. Pick two characters in the book. Set up a letter-writing correspondence of between two and four sets of letters written between them. Center the letter exchange on the turning point in the book.

40. Make a game based on the book's characters, theme, setting, mood, and information about the author.

41. Create a time line for the book. Stretch it out on a long, white sheet of paper, putting the dates and adding illustrations for each significant date on the time line.

42. Use a well-known quotation such as, "Youth is wasted on the young," by George B. Shaw or a proverb such as, "No use crying over spilt milk," that you think represents the main idea of the book and make a collage showing why this is so.

43. Play the role of a sage or wise person and write a letter to the main character advising him or her on how to deal with two other characters in the book.

44. Write a news or feature article on three important events in the book. Make a mock newspaper for your article. Make headlines to go along with your feature story.

45. Create a photo album using a series of four pictures to illustrate the main character(s), setting, plot, and your favorite part of the book. Write three to five descriptive sentences under each "photo."

"Novel" Photo Album

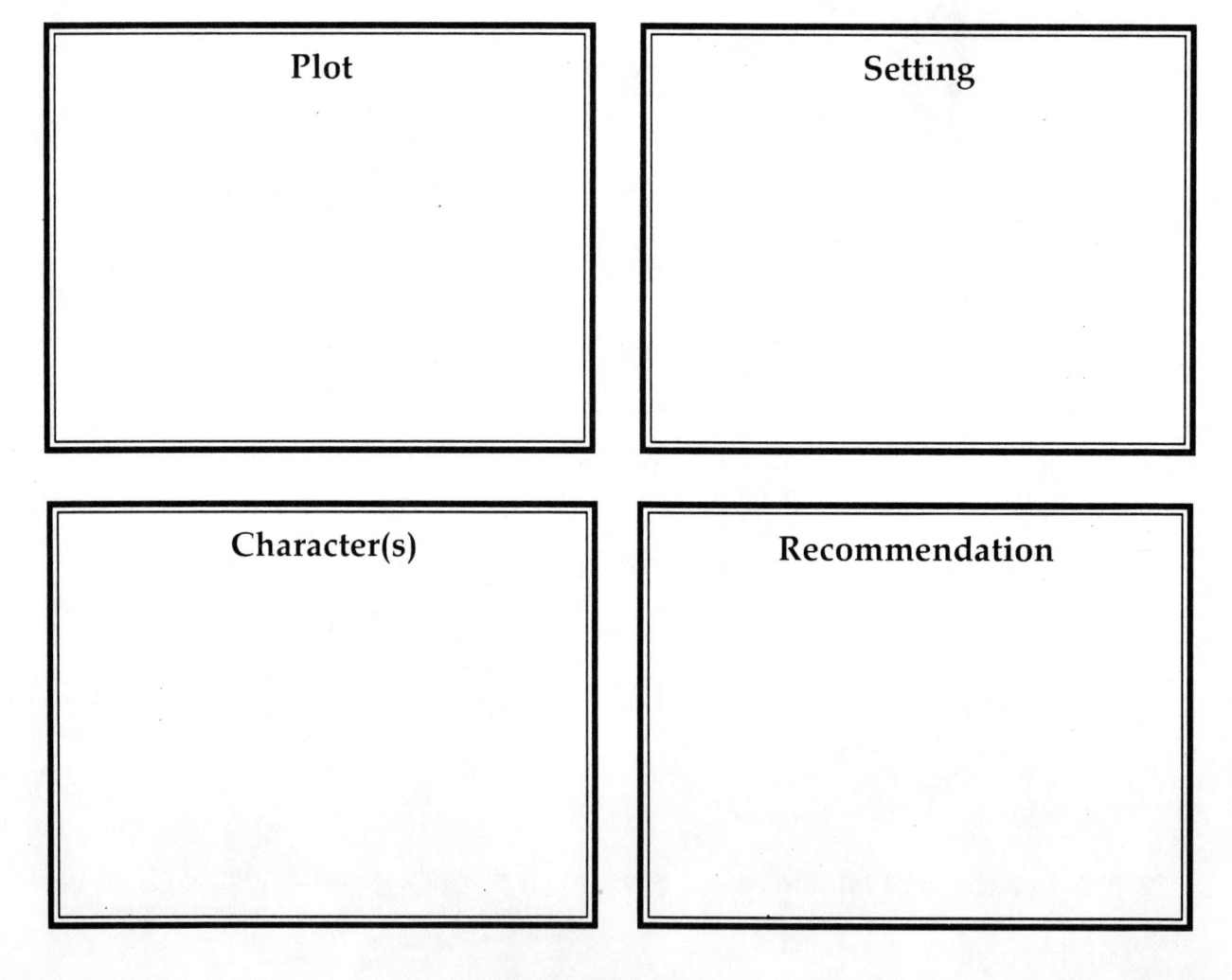

Plot	Setting

Character(s)	Recommendation

Now It's Your Turn

My Book Report Projects

1. The fiction book I plan to read is _____
   _____.

2. The author is _____
   _____.

3. The nonfiction book I plan to read is _____
   _____.

4. The author is _____
   _____.

5. My fiction book report project will be _____
   _____
   _____
   _____.

6. My nonfiction book report project will be _____
   _____
   _____
   _____.

Beautiful Banners

Banners have been popular throughout the ages. They were carried aloft by Roman legions, hoisted high by medieval knights, and are still popular with computer-age kids.

But banner making is more than dots or lines on the length of a computer printout. It is an ancient and noble art form which continues to delight makers and viewers alike. To make a banner you need a piece of stiff cloth, some squares of felt in contrasting colors, pieces of yarn, a jar of glue, a rod of wood, and a vivid imagination. Banners are a delightful way to highlight a report, to enhance a presentation, or to sell a school project. Below are some examples of banners you could use as models to design your own. It will just take a little time, ingenuity, and putting-it-together skills to create your own beautiful banner.

get into reading ... give your mind a fantasy flight

MATH
THE RIGHT ANGLE ON LIFE

PHYSICAL EDUCATION IS A LIFE SPORT.

ART
awesome silhouettes

Now It's Your Turn
My Banner

Now It's Your Turn
My Banner (cont'd.)

Creating Collages

Collage is a French word that means gluing or pasting. It is a wonderful art form in which materials are arranged, assembled, and pasted together to form a unique composition. To construct a collage, you need to gather a variety of materials: magazine pictures, photos, stamps, cloth, construction paper, colored cardboard, and miscellaneous objects. Then you need to plan your layout, so that the final product will do what you want it to do, say what you want it to say, or represent what you want it to represent.

First you cut out pictures, shapes, or symbols. Next you randomly arrange them and any other objects (buttons, concert tickets, receipts, etc.) on a piece of tagboard or thin plywood. After you are satisfied with the picture you have created, secure each item to the tagboard or plywood by gluing each item in place. The overall effect should be a free-form of varied color, different textures, and creative craftsmanship. Collages are fun to construct, impressive to see, and useful for reports. A sample collage follows.

Now It's Your Turn

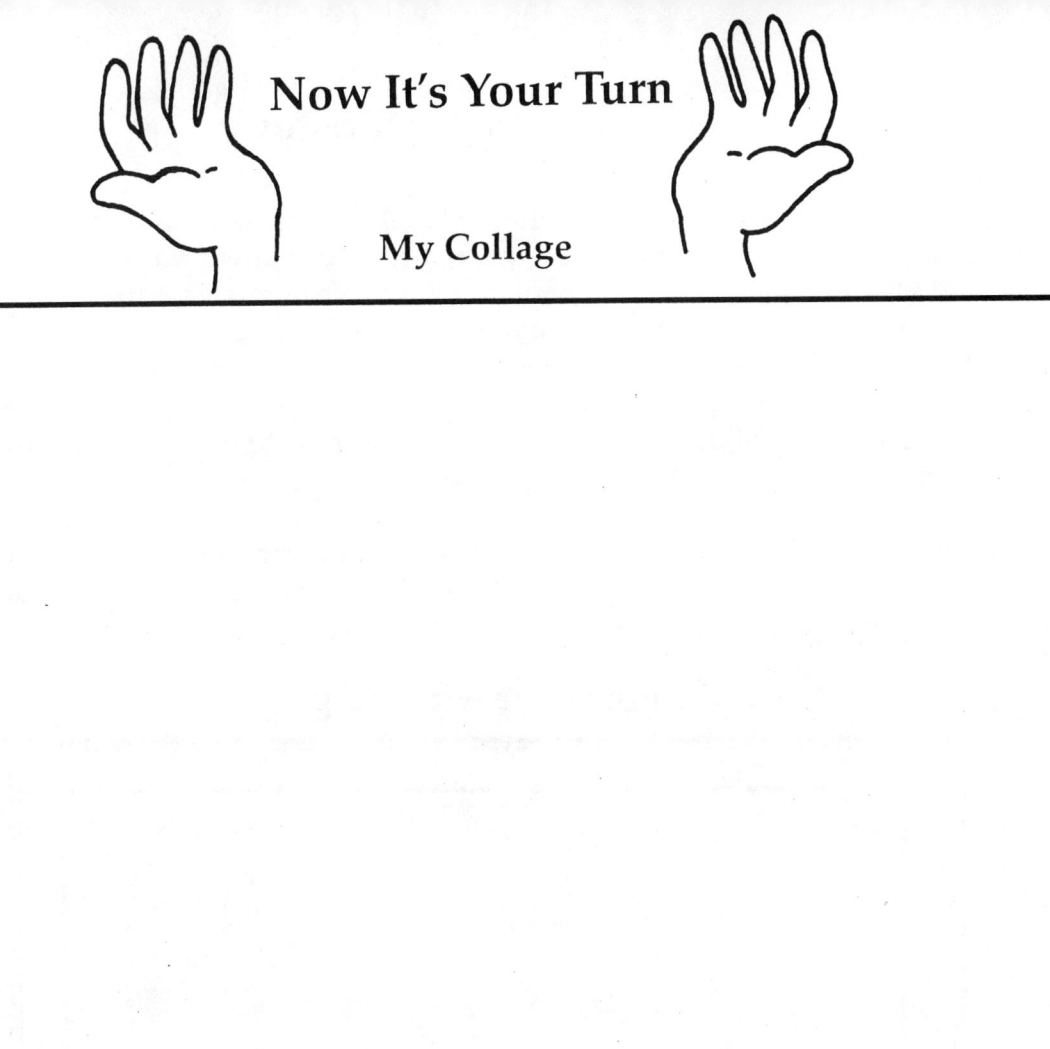

My Collage

How to Make a Poster

1. Plan your layout. Start your planning by looking through some magazines and examining the advertising products which attract your attention. Then ask yourself, "Why do I like these ads? What about them appeals to me? Is it the colors? Is it the way the objects in the advertisement are arranged? Is it the main image, letters, or the composition of the ad?" Use the characteristics you like in the ads to help you plan your poster and to help you make your poster appeal to an audience. A good "rule of thumb" to follow is to use an odd number of items. This tends to give it a good sense of balance or composition.

2. Next, create a picture frame around your poster. You can do this by placing a yardstick or ruler at the edge of your poster and drawing a light pencil line on all four sides. This will give your poster "space" in which you can work.

Picture Frame with Margins

3. Make the first drawing of your poster in pencil. Begin by centering your title. To do this, you need to count the number of letters you have in your title and find the middle. Keep in mind that spaces between words must be included in your title-letter count. Begin by writing the center letter in your title in the center of the poster. Continue to draw each letter from the center of the title to the left, and from the center of the title to the right. Just keep in mind that your title is limited to the amount of space you allowed in your predrawn picture frame (see sample above).

If your title is "The History of Rock Music," (which has 25 spaces) the center is *o* in the word *of*. The easiest way to explain the idea of centering your title is to show you an example:

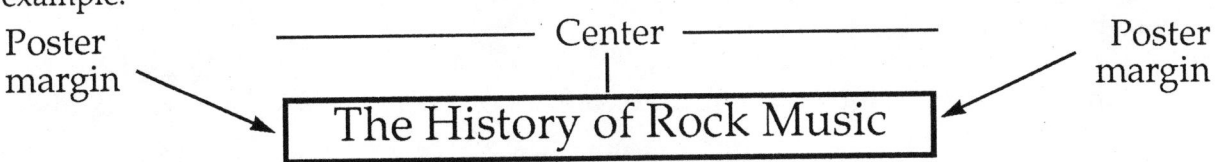

Poster margin ──────── Center ──────── Poster margin

| The History of Rock Music |

4. Use pencil to make your first drawing of images or spaces for pictures. If you are using photocopies, postcards, or pictures cut from magazines, move them about on your poster to get a good feeling for what your poster will look like when you are finished with it. The overall goal is to have a poster that is artistically arranged and visually satisfying.

5. After you are satisfied with the picture you have planned, go over the pencil border lines with bold markers or bold-colored pencils, remembering that any color you put on your poster should be dark enough to be seen from across the room. After you have finished your poster, put it at one end of the room, walk to the opposite end of the room, and see how well your poster can be seen from the distance. If you cannot see everything on your poster, you know your audience won't be able to see everything on it either. One further bit of advice is, do not use yellow in the title and limit its use on most parts of your poster because yellow tends to wash out at any distance.

6. Before your poster is finalized, check to see if it needs to be *tidied* in any way. Erase any unnecessary pencil marks, clear up any smudges, etc. Then make sure that everything appears to be straight or properly aligned on your poster.

7. Now that you have taken the time to design an effective tool (your poster) for your presentation, practice using it. Find an audience who will listen to your speech to offer suggestions on how well you present your topic and for how you might make your presentation even better.

8. You might find it useful to tape-record your report, play it back for yourself, and hear how you sound to others.

9. Just keep in mind that when you are giving a presentation to a group, your goal is to sell them your topic. To do this use all the tricks you can think of to make your report interesting, informative, and entertaining.

10. Don't forget to put your name, date, and (perhaps) class period on the back of your poster before you bring it to class for your presentation.

11. Finally, remember any job worth doing is worth doing well. Posters are an art form.

S
A
M
P
L
E

P
O
S
T
E
R

Now It's Your Turn

My Poster

Making Mobiles

One of the most effective visuals you can make is a mobile. A mobile is easy to construct, fun to make, and wonderful to view by an audience. To make a mobile, all you need is some kind of building material such as construction paper, tagboard, metal, wood, glass, paper, or plastic; some means by which to add color such as paint, markers, or colored pencils; some way to affix objects to your project such as wire, thread, string, fishing line, glue, or rubber cement; and, of course, your imagination.

The most important element in making a mobile is that you make it so that it can move; after all, the word *mobile* means movable. Not only should your mobile move, but it should give pleasure, visual appeal, and purpose to your presentation or demonstration.

A mobile consists of various objects designed to balance and move independently of one another. The objects you select to attach to your mobile are limitless. They can be abstract, geometrical, or three-dimensional. There are no hard and fast rules for making a mobile. Generally, though, mobiles are made from the bottom up. That means that you start by assembling the lower portion first and finish by assembling the top portion. To attach objects to the mobile, punch holes in the top of the objects and loop thread or string through the holes, and tie a knot in the thread or string. Next punch a hole in the bottom portion of the object to which you want to attach another object. Keep in mind that the point of balance is the center of the mobile. (See examples of mobiles on the following pages.)

Once you have finished constructing your mobile, you will want to hang it. Hang your mobile where there is a slight draft or breeze so that it will float freely and sway in the wind.

Making Mobiles

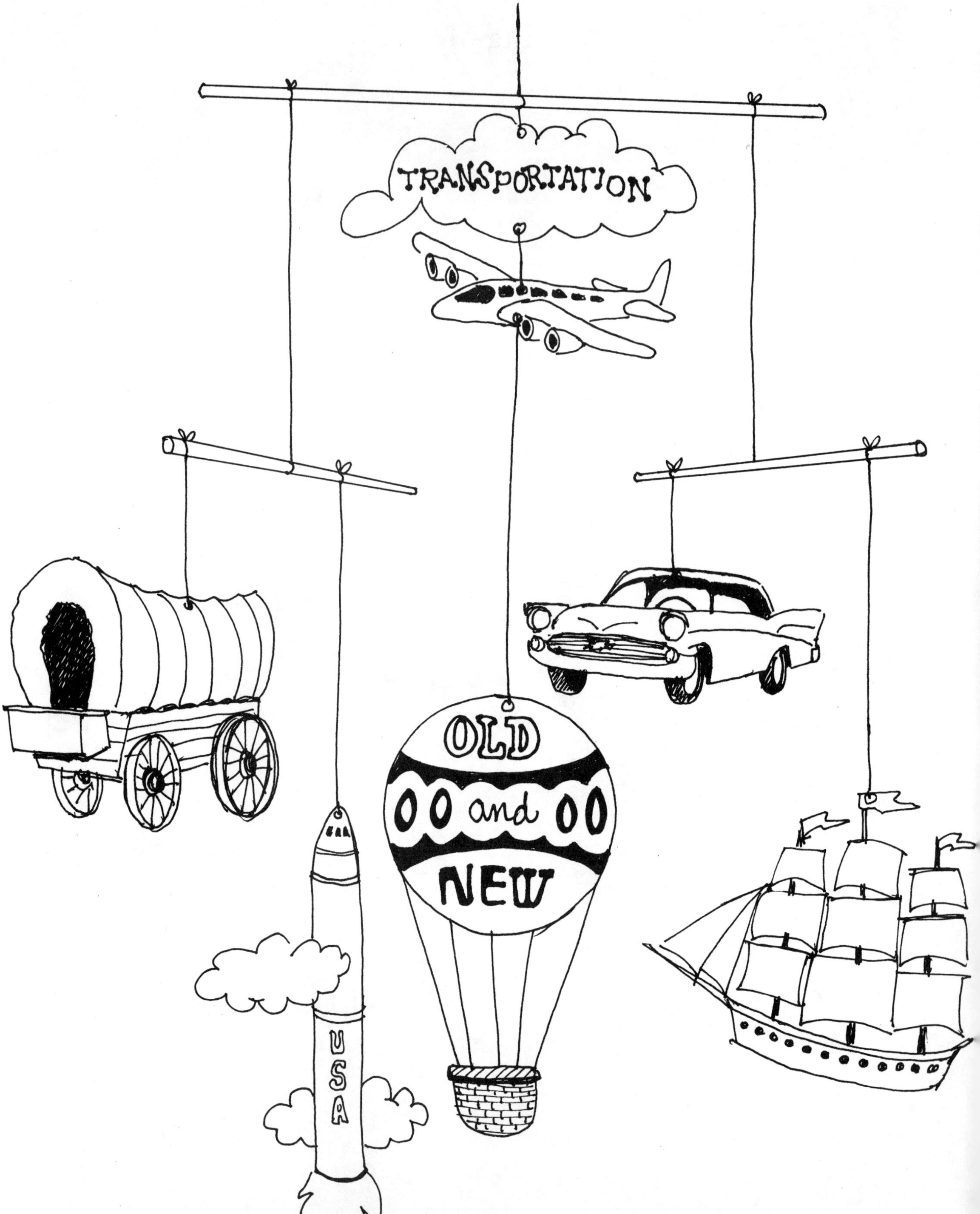
TRANSPORTATION
OLD
and
NEW
USA

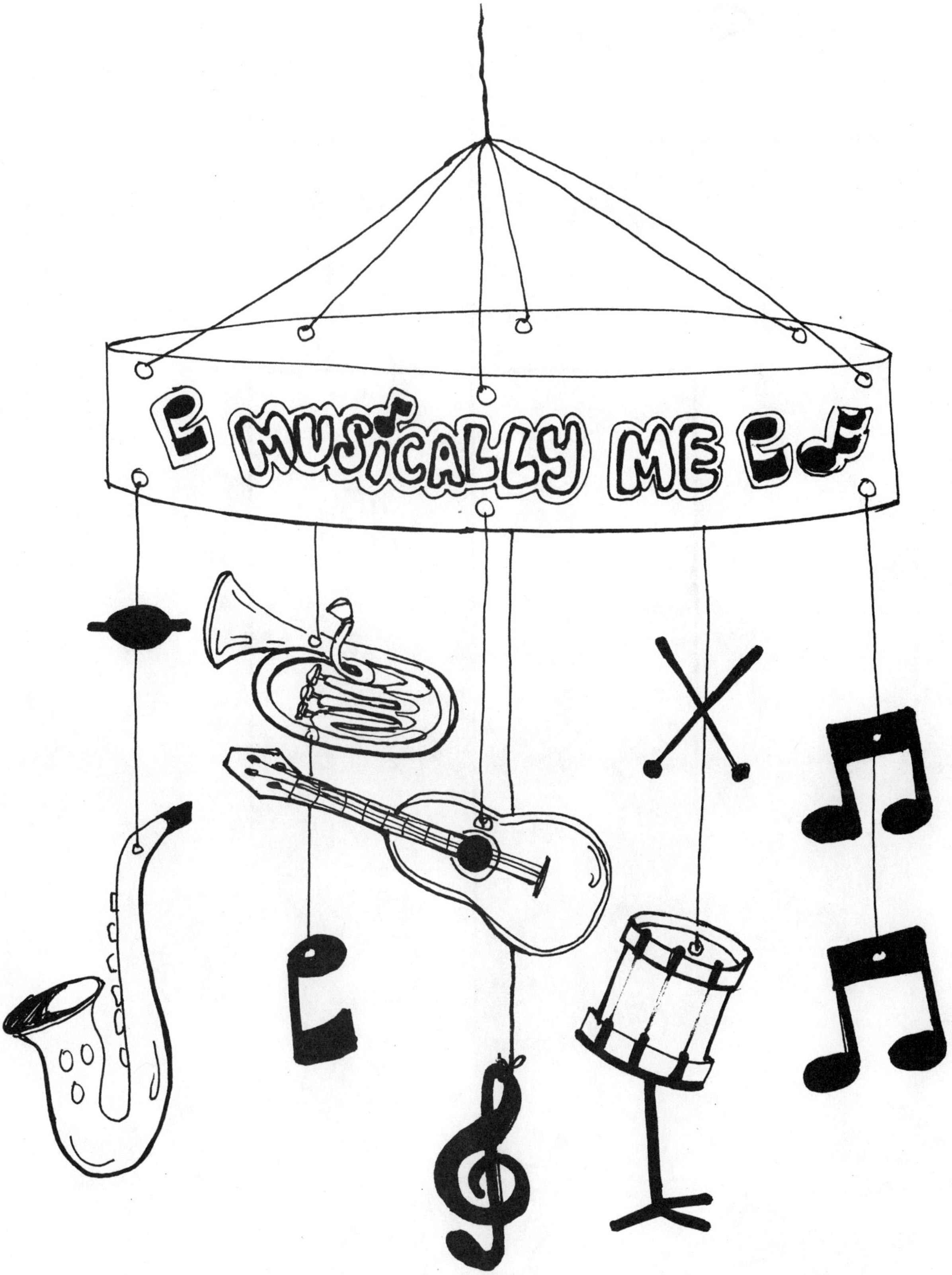
MUSICALLY ME

Now It's Your Turn

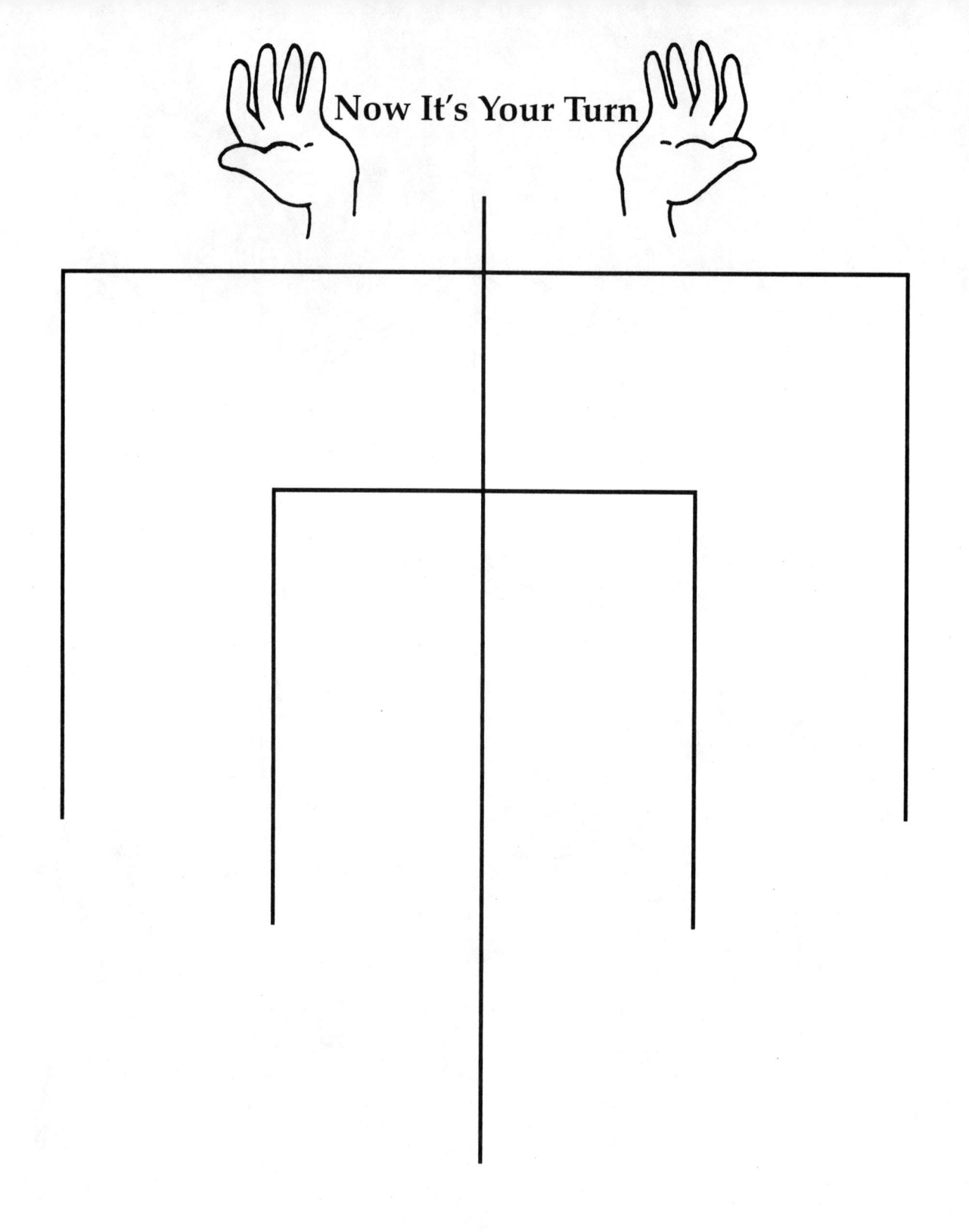

Now It's Your Turn

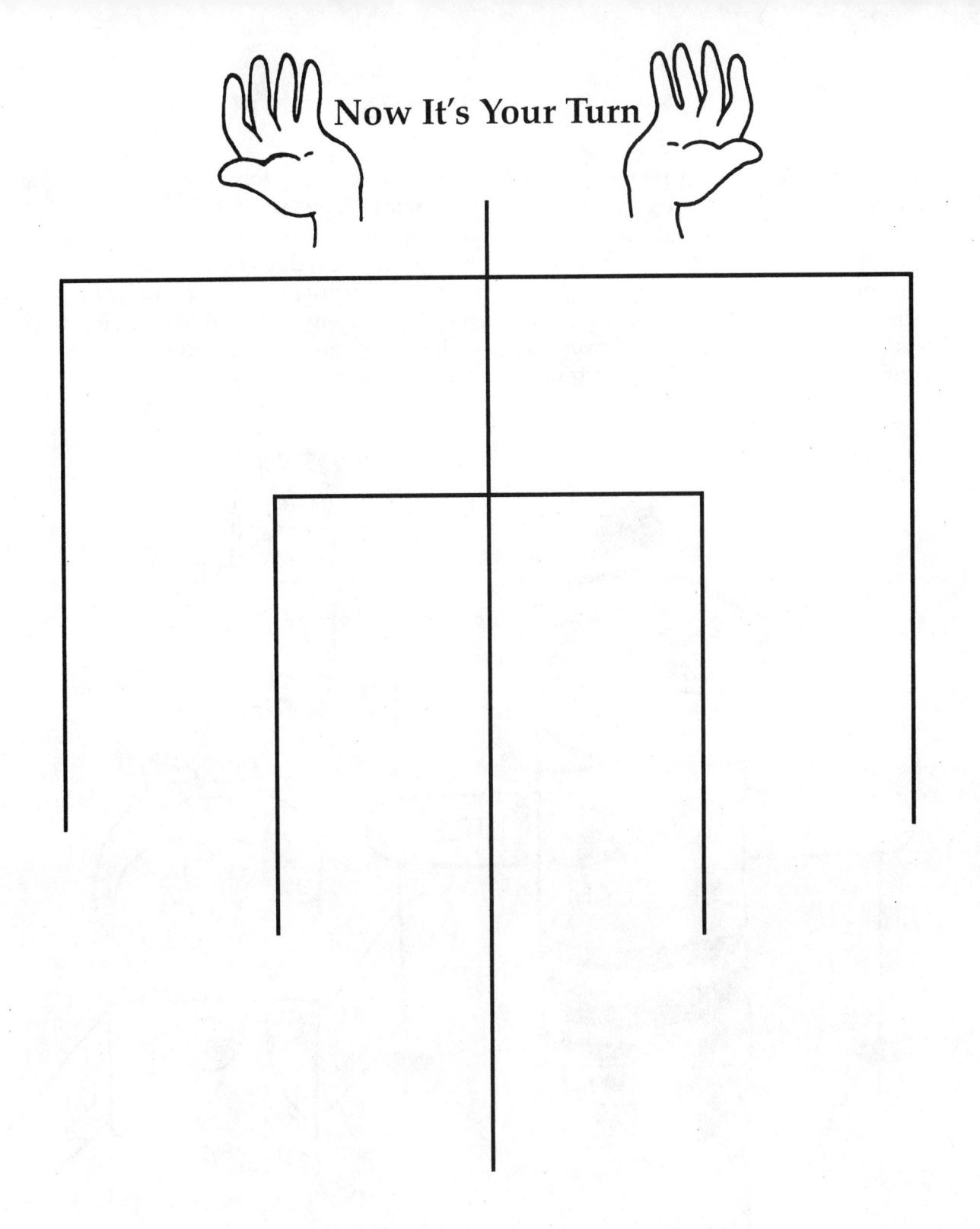

Puppet People

Pioneer children owned few, if any, store-bought toys. They took delight in making their toys from "found objects" in their environment. They cut willow whistles, whittled boxes and windmills, and made rag-doll puppets to fill their precious moments when they were not needed to help their parents with everyday chores. Today, you can carry on the pioneer tradition of creating your own puppet people. By following the examples shown below and using the pattern provided, you will be able to design puppets for book reports, research projects, class demonstrations, or for your own amusement. Remember to decorate the front and back sides of your puppet.

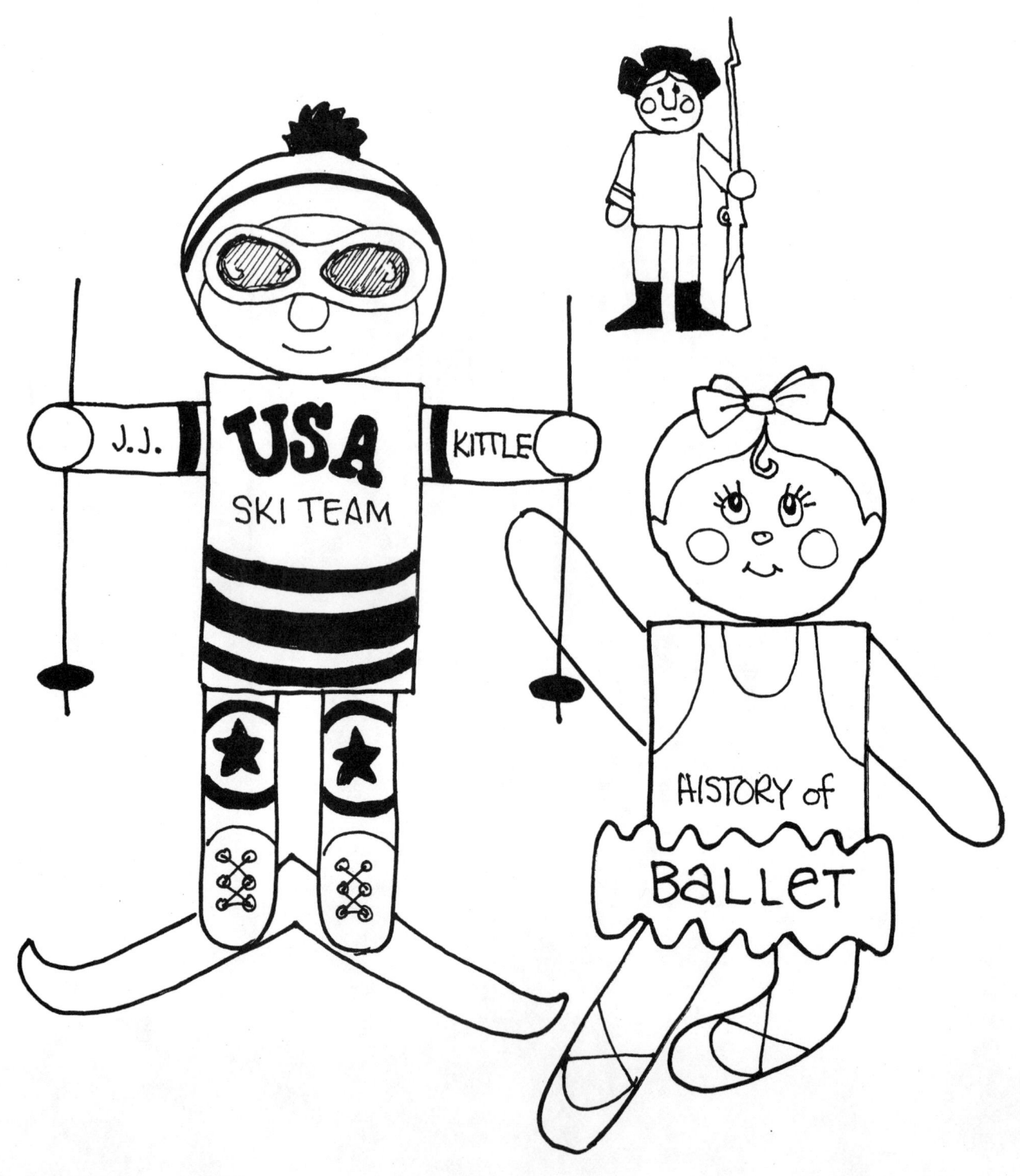

Now It's Your Turn
My Puppet

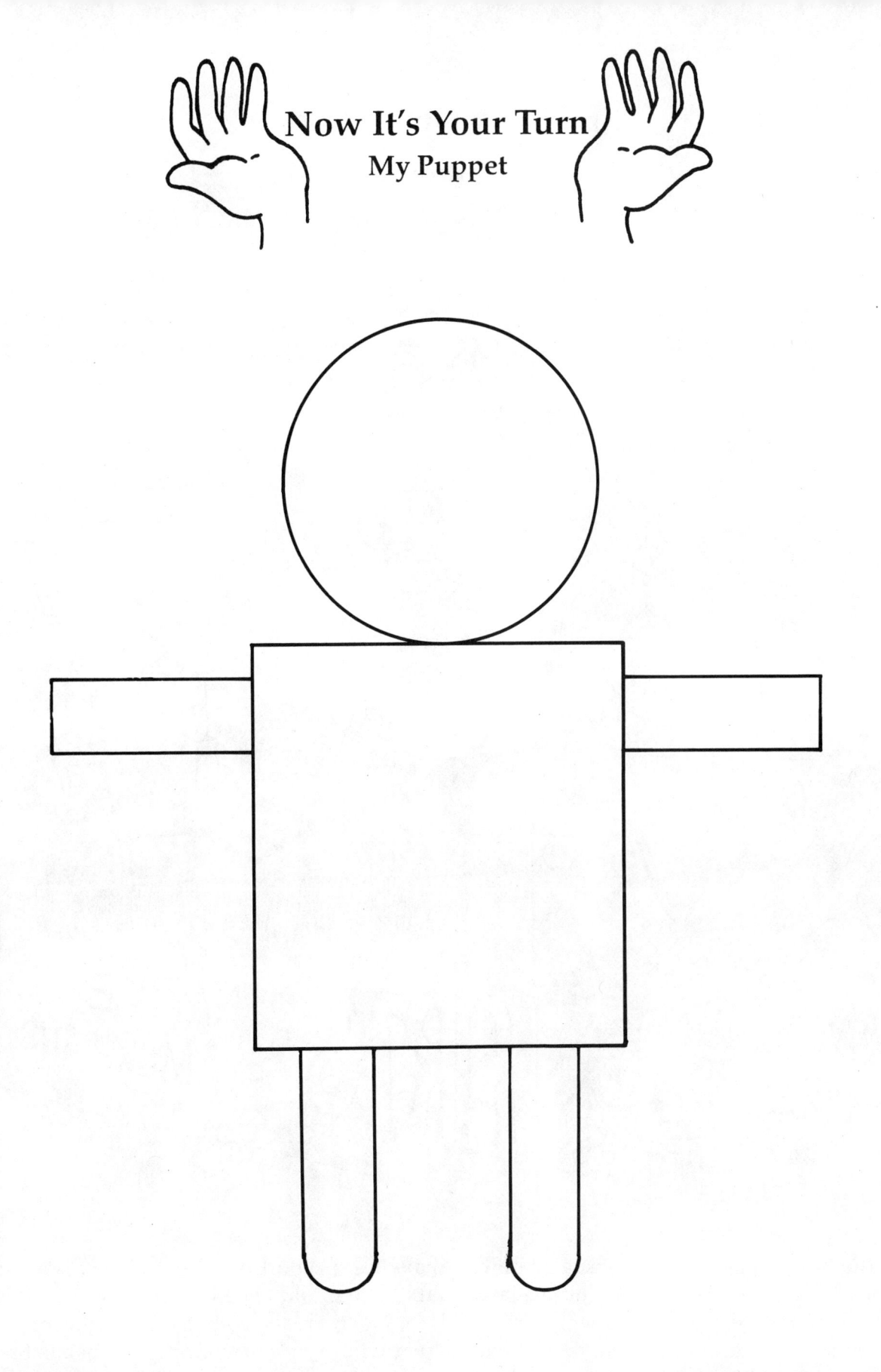

115

Shoe Box Float Projects

One of the most effective visuals you can make for a report or school project is a shoe box float. The directions are quite simple. First, get an old shoe box and cover it on all sides with construction paper, paint, or cloth. Next, create your own, or find objects around the house to put on your "float" which will represent your report theme. Shoe box floats work well for science projects, social studies presentations, book reports, foreign language activities, or other subject topics. When each student in the class makes a float, it would be fun to invite parents, staff, and other students to see the "floats on parade." Each float owner should give a running commentary about his or her float.

Now It's Your Turn
My Shoe Box Float

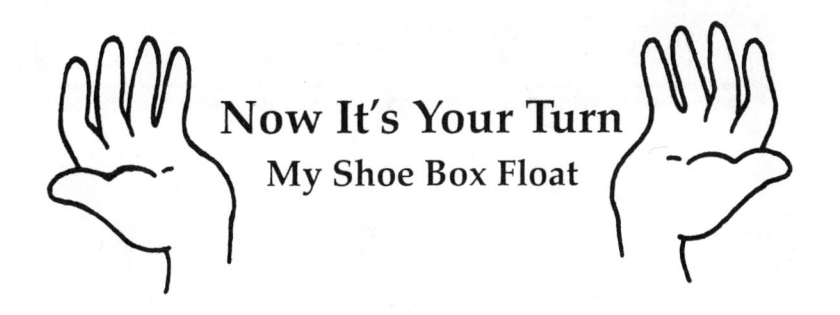

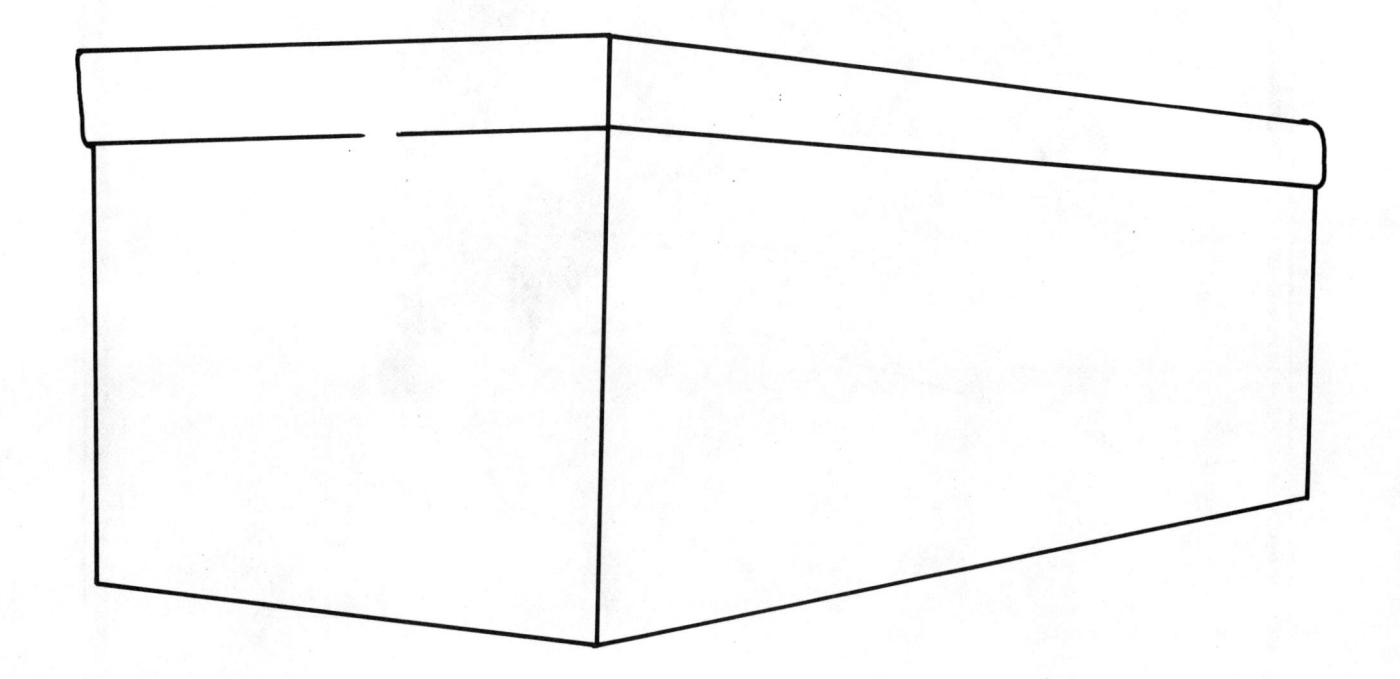

Poetry gives voice to our

silent songs.

The Language of Poets and Poetry

The famous British writer Lord Byron said of poetry that "the best poetry will be found to have power of forming, sustaining, and delighting us, as nothing else can." What strong words he has used to describe poetry, and what strong powers do Byron's words impart to poets. Poetry is special because it touches the soul deep inside each of us. Poetry can bring us to tears due to the grief or joy we find in it, and in fact, there is a poet deep inside each of us waiting to be released, waiting to express our thoughts, aspirations, and delights we find in the world around us, in our fellow human beings.

Some students think that poetry is only for those who care about blooming flowers or being in love, but poetry is all about life. It is about a baseball game, a grandparent, a warm summer day; it is about human things. As a child, you were probably enchanted by hearing Mother Goose rhymes, and in no time at all you could recite them by heart. Now that you are more mature, you can enjoy poetry because of its language, its repetitions, its sounds, its rhythms, its images, and most of all its meaning.

LORD BYRON

Poetry should be read silently and read out loud to get its full flavor. The more poems you read, the more you will see how appealing they are. The poems of Jack Prelutsky, Shel Silverstein, David McCord, and Dr. Seuss will amuse you with their enchanting rhymes, made-up words, and fanciful farces. Whereas the poems of Nikki Giovanni, Langston Hughes, Robert Frost, Carl Sandburg, X.J. Kennedy, and Gwendolyn Brooks will make you sit up and take notice of what it's like to grow up as a Black American or Hispanic in America; what it was like living in Chicago (or any large urban center) in the early 1900s; or what it is like "Stopping by Woods on a Snowy Evening." Poetry is not intended to be dissected, analyzed, or memorized in meaningless ways. It is intended to make you see, hear, taste, and feel in a way prose can never make you see, hear, taste, or feel. Poetry gives sound to silent songs.

The Language of Poets and Poetry

Before you examine different poetic forms and different poetic formulas, you need to keep in mind that the most important characteristic of good poetry is that it must say something fresh. Poetry should leave the reader with a sense of *wow*! While there are terms to be studied and formulas to follow, poetry should never be ordinary or commonplace; it should be the opportunity to give voice to silent songs.

Poets have their own jargon or specialized language in which they "talk to one another" in order to have a mutual understanding. While you don't need to know all the jargon of poetry in order to write poetry, it goes without saying that the more language you know about anything, the better you are able to communicate in the jargon of that field. Listed below are definitions and examples of many poetic terms. By studying the language of poetry and modeling student examples, you should be inspired to explore the "language of poets" and write many kinds of poems yourself.

1. **Alliteration** is the repetition of consonant sounds at the beginning, middle, or end of a line of poetry.

    - Creamy, crunchy, crispy treats called me to the kitchen.
    - The soft, sweet sound of Cynthia's voice.
        —Mike Julian
    - Sarah swims slowly, silently, and softly.
        —Holly Bierbaum

2. **Apostrophe** is a figure of speech in which a thing, place, or idea is addressed as if it were capable of understanding.

    - Bright, old, moon dreams dreams of yesteryear.
    - Silver-green cacti sang songs to silent sands.
    - Purple mountains silently sleep through the blizzard.

3. **Assonance** is the repetition of vowel sounds.

    - Allison ate an appetizing apple.
        —Kevin Rischow
    - Ishi eyed the enemy, anticipating an attack.

4. **Caesura** is a pause within a line of poetry which is indicated by a double line (//).

    - Cover his face // my eyes daze // he died too young.
        —Kevin Rischow
    - Freedom // how I long for thee.
        —C. Luckman

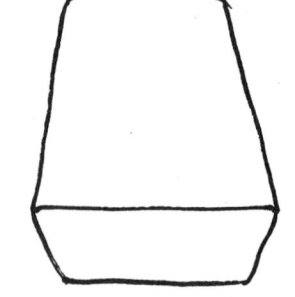

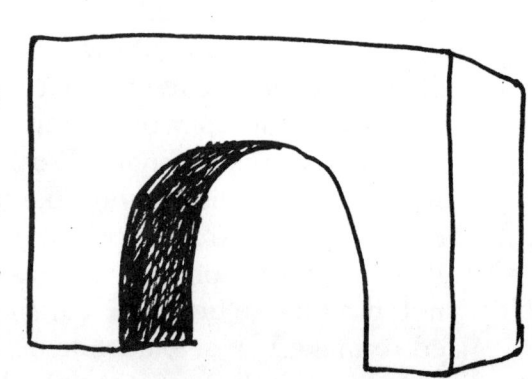

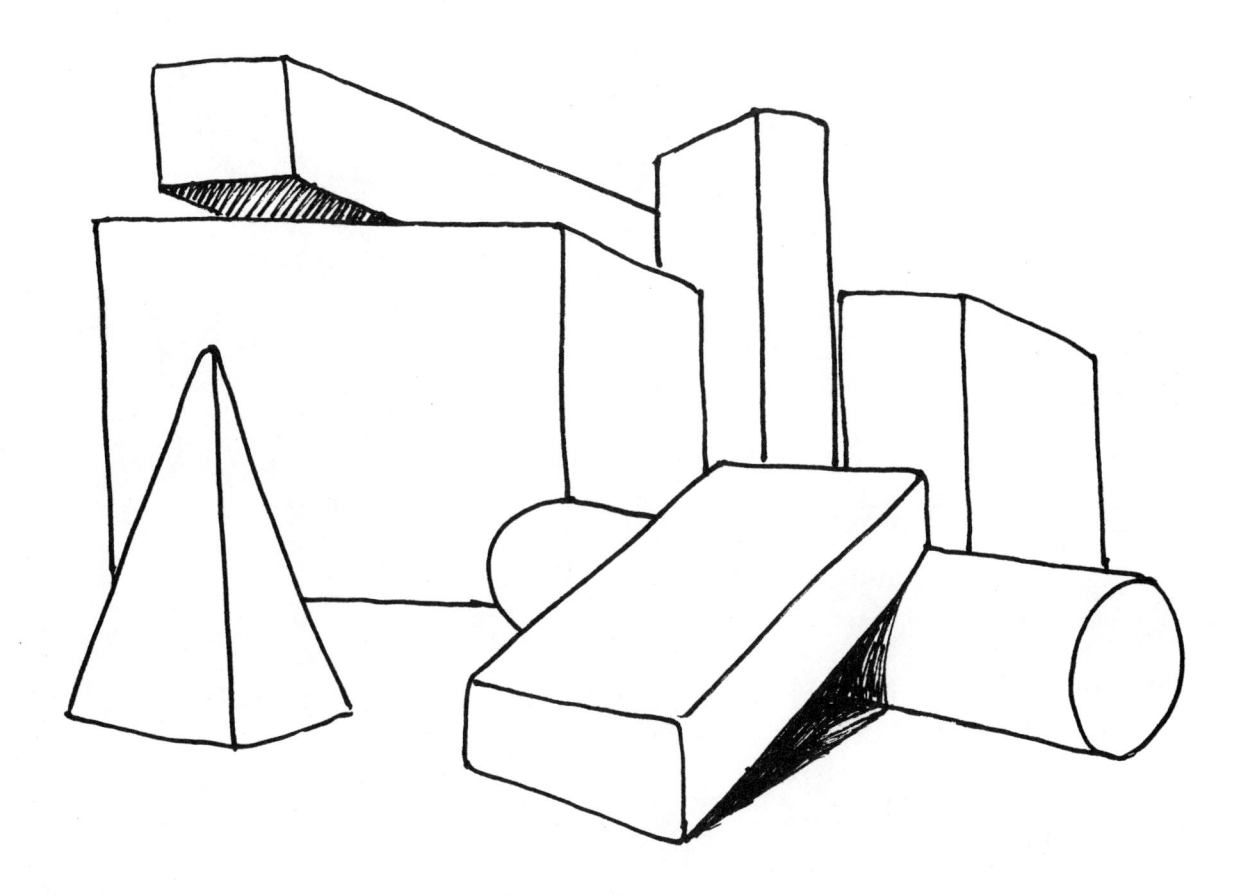

5. **Connotation** is the meaning attached to a word beyond its dictionary definition. For example, the words *stingy, penny-pinching, close-fisted, frugal, cheap, petty,* and *thrifty* mean about the same thing. But the words give us different feelings. You would be pleased if people referred to you as *frugal*, whereas you would be insulted if they called you *cheap*. Words are very potent and should be used carefully so that the messages you intend your words to convey are the messages the reader gets from them. Examples of word connotations follow.

- *Yankee* is a word that will mean different things if you live in New England, in the South, or in a foreign country.

- *Thin, skinny, gawky, scrawny, slender,* and *bony* all have about the same dictionary meaning, but no doubt you would prefer being called *thin* or *skinny*, rather than being referred to as *scrawny* or *bony*.

- Think of the differences attached to these words: *job, chore, assignment, task, work, duty,* or *stint*. Some of the words are positive in tone while others are negative.

6. **Denotation** is the dictionary meaning of a word.

- The government was *toppled* by the dissatisfied citizens.

- The *grandeur* of the place was widely accepted by tourists.

7. **Hyperbole** is an exaggeration or overstatement used to get the reader's attention.

   - My dad had a cow when he saw my grades!
   - I'll remember you forever.
   - He ate like a hippo.

8. **Image/Imagery** is a mental picture created by what is written.

   - The rookie baseball player slid across the plate in a haze of gray smoke. "You're out!" screamed the ump, as the dust died around the lad.
   - Seared by the sun on a hot, summer's day . . . .

9. **Irony** is deliberately saying the opposite of what is meant. However, it is not intended to hurt.

   - The fire-engulfed, egg factory's delightful odor drifted across the surrounding countryside.
   - My favorite Friday afternoon pastime is cleaning my room, taking out the trash, and mowing the lawn.

10. **Metaphor** is a figure of speech that makes a comparison between two unrelated things without using *like* or *as* in the comparison.

    - The history test was a disaster.
    - The substitute teacher in math class was a real clown.
    - My neighbor is a pig.

11. **Meter** is the rhythm in a poem which is caused by stressed, accented or long syllables and unstressed, unaccented or short syllables (the stressed syllables are italicized).

    - There *once* was a *man* from Cape *Cod*
      Who *rode* his *steed* to Fort *Dodge*.
    - 'Twas the *night* before *Christ*mas, . . .
    - *Double*, double, *toil* and *trouble*,
      Fire burn and *caul*dron *bubble*.

12. **Onomatopoeia** is the use of words that sound like the action they represent.

    - Buzz, bark, pitter-patter, woosh, honk, bang

    - Echo, crash, babble, zigzag, splash, quack

13. **Personification** is a figure of speech that gives life to inanimate objects.

    - The sun tangoed among the clouds.

    - The car's engine whistled a capella after its long overdue tune-up.

    - The hands of the clock ached as time dallied toward midnight.

14. **Poetry** is natural language which enables a writer to express thoughts in verse rather than in prose. It is the dance of a pen, the waltz of words, the breath of life. Poetry, properly written and read, is as tasty as eating, as tuneful as music, and as powerful as the ancient Roman Empire. Poetry gives meaning to our lives.

15. **Rhyme** (also spelled rime) is when the words in a poem have the same or similar sounds. True rhymes consist of identical sounding syllables. For example, *fun* and *run* are true rhymes, but all rhyming words do not need to be true rhymes to function in poetry. Rhyming words often appear at the ends of lines of poetry, but they may also fall within the lines, and when they do they are called internal rhyming words. A good example of internal rhyme is seen in Edgar Allen Poe's famous poem "The Raven." He wrote: "Once upon a midnight *dreary*, while I pondered, weak and *weary*, . . ." A point to remember is that rhyming words are often used in poetry, but good rhyming words must be "natural" and "honest;" they must not be "forced" or "dishonest." You might find a rhyming dictionary helpful in creating rhyming patterns in your poetry.

    - The toys at the end of the *shelves*,
      were made by Santa's little *elves*.

    - She ran as fast as she *could*,
      leaving us awestruck where we *stood*.

16. **Rhythm** is the beat of a poem. It is caused by the use of stressed and unstressed syllables. Rhythm gives a poem its tempo.
    - . . . *make* of *it*, *take* of *it* . . . .
    - The *ice* was *here*, the *ice* was *here*, the *ice* was all *around*.

17. **Simile** is a comparison of two things using the words *like* or *as*.
    - The vines were like golden chains around the flower's stem.
    - The old boots looked as though they had been through a desert storm.

18. **Stanza** is the division of a poem based on the number of lines it has. Stanzas are the "paragraphs" of poems. Often each new line of the poem begins with a capital letter.
    - A couplet (like a couple) has two lines in each stanza.
    - A triplet (like a trio) has three lines in each stanza.
    - A quatrain (like a quarter) has four lines in each stanza.

Quatrain
Bs are bad.
Cs are worse.
Ds and Fs
Are always cursed.

19. **Symbol/Symbolism** is a concrete or real object that is used to represent an idea. Symbols are used to refer to things beyond themselves.
    - A flag is a symbol of a nation, team, organization.
    - A bird is a symbol of flight, of freedom.
    - Green symbolizes prosperity, vegetation, greed.
    - A jaguar symbolizes speed and endurance.

20. **Verse** is the name for a line of traditional poetry written in meter. It is a synonym for stanza.
    - Monometer is a one-foot line.
    - Dimeter is a two-foot line.
    - Trimeter is a three-foot line.

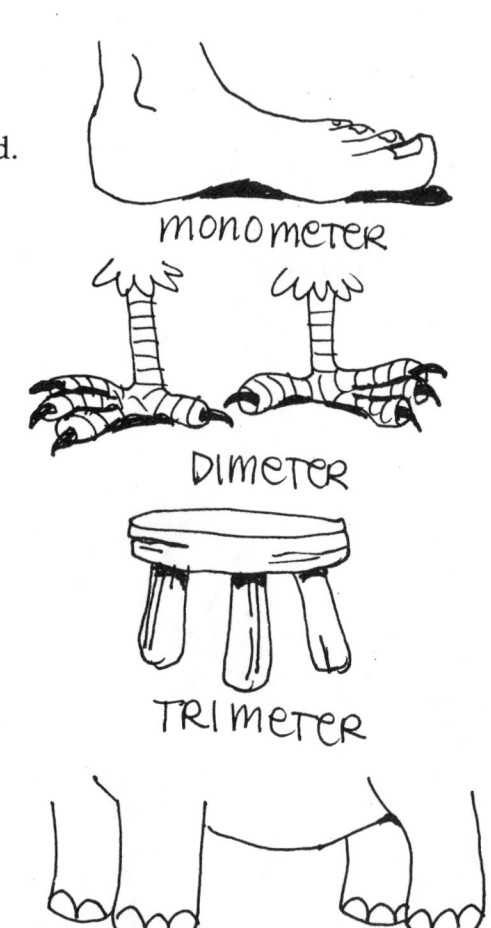

Now It's Your Turn

Using the definitions and models for the language of poetry, create your own examples for each.

1. alliteration: _____

2. apostrophe: _____

3. assonance: _____

4. connotation: _____

5. denotation: _____

6. hyperbole: _____

7. image/imagery: _____

8. irony: _____

9. metaphor: _____

10. onomatopoeia: _____

11. personification: _____

12. rhyme: _____

13. simile: _____

14. symbol: _____

Haiku, Cinquain, Acrostic, Free Verse, and Limerick

Learning to write different kinds of poetry is like going on an archaeological dig. Once you get beneath a layer of soil, there is no telling what wonders might come to the surface to reveal nature's beauty, to celebrate a friendship, to strike out in protest, to recall a loved one who has died, or to enable you to help us understand one of life's mysteries in a fresh, new light. Writing poetry and discovering different kinds of poetry can enable you to do just those things. Like the archaeologist going beneath the "skin of the earth" to reveal many marvelous treasures, writing a variety of poems will free you to see the world around you in a new perspective. So get your "trowel," your scratch pad, your precision measuring tools, and let's go on a "dig," a poetic one at that. We'll begin our journey of investigation in the East.

Haiku originated in Japan in the thirteenth century. It is composed of three lines totaling seventeen syllables in a 5, 7, 5 pattern. It is a short, focused poem, centered around one image or picture. In recent years it has become very popular with American teachers and their students, but true haiku, written by the masters like Bashô or Issa are not easy to write, and sometimes they are not easy to understand. Traditional haiku is unrhymed, its themes are nature (rather than human nature) or one of the four seasons, and the poem refers to a particular event (last night's full moon), not to a general event (any full moon). While most of the haiku written by American students today is not really haiku, it is nevertheless fun to try your hand at this kind of aesthetic poetry.

Haiku

Fragile daffodils
Herald spring, golden trumpets
Stand silently tall

The Parrot

Bright colored feathers
With bits of turquoise and red
Flutter in the air.
   Christin Luckman

Deer eat the soft moss
In the cave near the new springs.
Nature surrounds them.
   Mike Julian

Blowing in the night
The trees shake furiously
When will the storm stop?
   Adrienne White

Cinquain is a five-line poem created by Adelaide Crapsey in 1911. She was fluent in French and used the French word *cinq* as the basis for her five-lined poems.

Line 1: Title	Pine pillars
Line 2 Description of title	Sleek emerald gemstones
Line 3: Action about the title	Sheltering cardinals
Line 4: Feeling about the title	Warmly welcoming winter
Line 5: Synonym for title	Evergreens

Moon
Aloft, silent
Revolves, brightens, darkens
Inspiring, poetic, illuminating, lyrical
Beacon

Anonymous

Water
Loud, active
Shallows, deepens, swallows
Scary, poetic, noisy, beautiful
Ocean

Mike Gerbec

Metamorphosis
Transformation, variation
Alteration, mutation, modification
Amazement, confusion, wonder, excitement
Change

Justin Schwartz

Acrostics are "formula" poems in which the first line begins with the first letter of a word spelled vertically. Often people will use their names as the basis of their poem; however, animals, friendship, or any topic is suitable for an acrostic. Examples follow.

Brawny, brazen, architect
Oversees sturdy, city strongholds
Bronzed, edifaces, urban-chateaux

Dancing, swimming, gleefully, gliding
Occasionally dreaming in summer's sweet light.
Lingering as ships sail on by
Popping up and out of the sea
Habitually helping other creatures
Interesting to humans one and all
Never really scared until harm comes their way

    Heather Brooks

Baseball is my favorite sport
Red is my favorite color
Interesting person that I am
Amazing even myself at times
Never one who likes to be left out.

    Brian Faber

Summer is a special time
Underneath the tree's shade
Music from an ice cream truck
Making its way into my
Ears. School is over, finally I can
Rest.

    Sean Nicol

Free Verse is poetry which does not have a syllable count, rhyming pattern, or pre-ordained formula. It is the favorite form of many poets because it gives poets the greatest freedom to express themselves, to share their ideas, or to stand up to the silence of their lives. But free-verse poets must offer the reader music, joy, surprise. The poem must matter in some way, or it is mere rambling, not a poem.

The Roaring River and My Two Dogs

The river roared as the storm came about,
but stupid ol' me let my dogs go out.
Not knowing what I had done until a crash
of thunder rocked the house,
I ran outside without a cover
Whistling and yelling my old dogs' names,
not knowing where, then I heard a yelp
fill the air. I couldn't see 'em, then a flash
of lightning led the way. I came down to the river
only to see my dogs swimming the other way.
I took a dive into the cold, roaring river and swam
to the sides of my dogs, they could barely breathe.
I got one and took him to shore. I plunged in for the other,
but she was headed the other way.
At last I reached her, sleek as an eel, impossible
to grab on to, I couldn't get a grip 'round her.
Fighting the current, but carefully holding on,
as her litter was due a week from tomorrow.
When we reached the shore, she hardly moved at all.
I scooped her up in my arms and carried her
the whole way home, hoping no harm had come to her
or her family-to-be. I built a warm, roaring fire
and laid both dogs beside it. The orange-red flames
warmed their soaked coats. At length, both dogs were dry,
up and about, and a week later there were puppies, puppies all about.

   Frank Ross

Baseball

The crack of the bat
the smell of peanuts
the noisy fans
the sight of green grass
the catcher flashing signals.
Baseball.

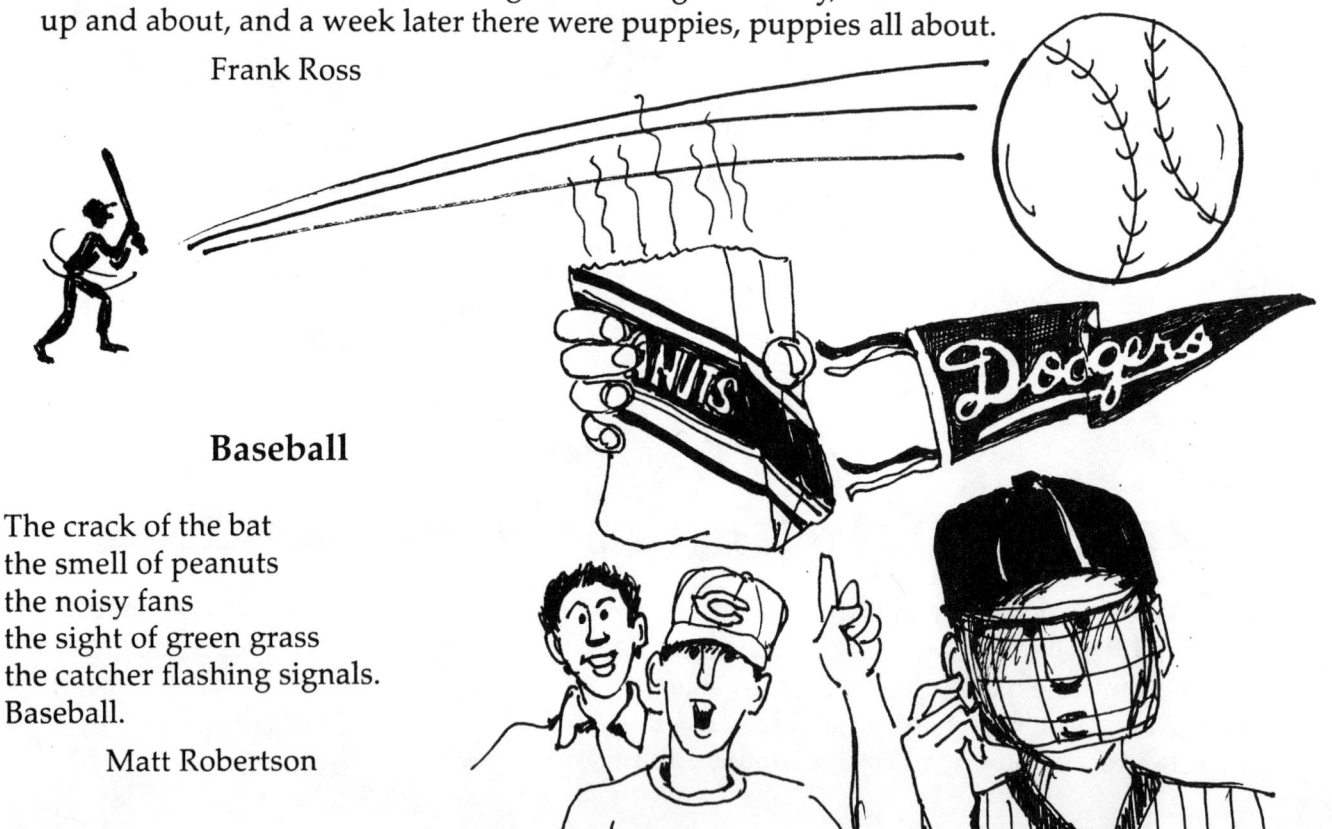

  Matt Robertson

Moving

I remember we listed our house in May,
I had mixed feelings about moving away.

We lived in our home for about ten years.
The thought of leaving brought me to tears.

New friends, new school, and a new home,
A whole new place, I'd be so alone.

The day we moved out it was pouring rain,
I'd said to myself, "I will no longer complain."

This moving experience was good for me,
It wasn't as bad as I pictured it to be.

        Mike Missak

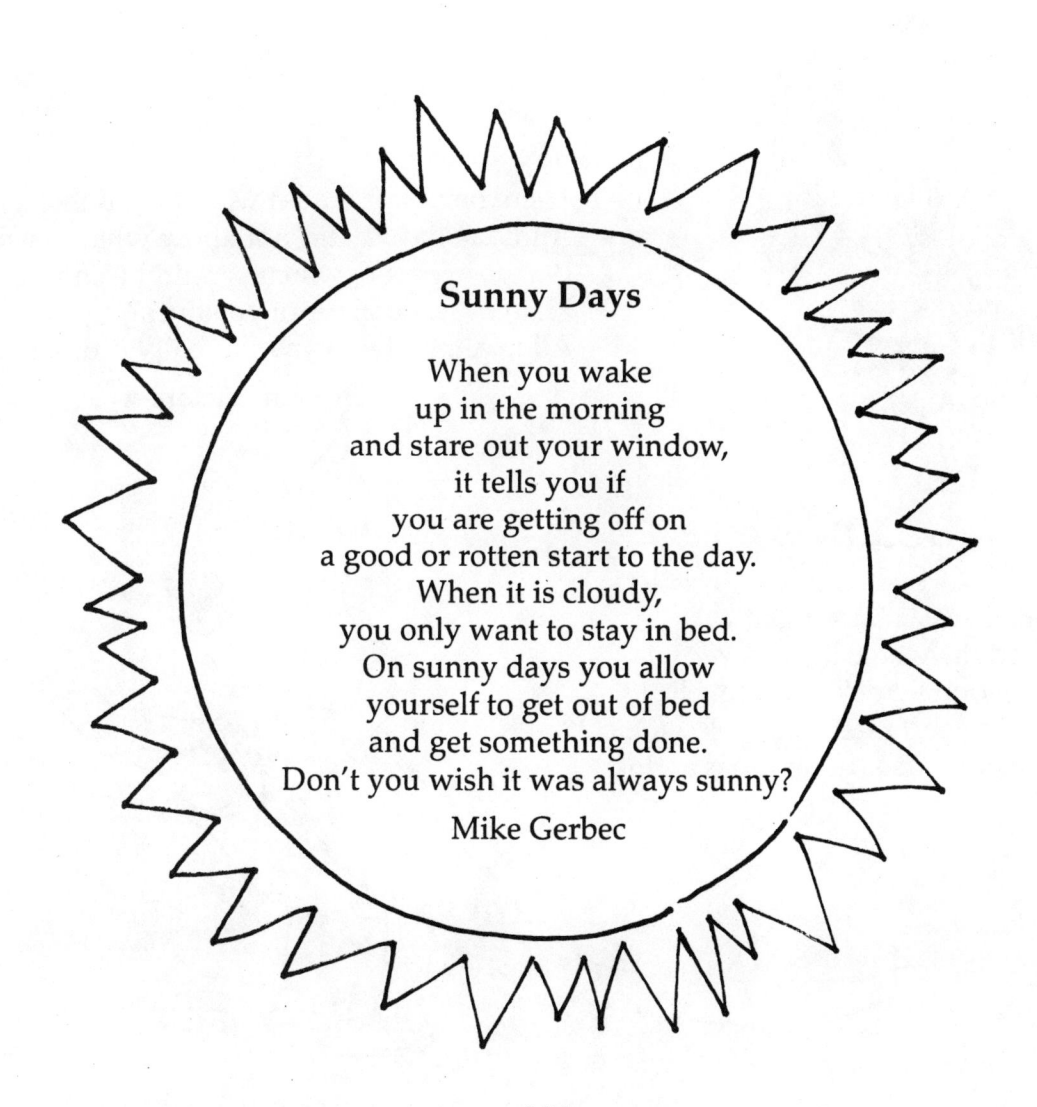

Sunny Days

When you wake
up in the morning
and stare out your window,
it tells you if
you are getting off on
a good or rotten start to the day.
When it is cloudy,
you only want to stay in bed.
On sunny days you allow
yourself to get out of bed
and get something done.
Don't you wish it was always sunny?

        Mike Gerbec

A **limerick** is a humorous five-line poem that was made into a wonderful art form by the master of limerick, Edward Lear, who is often referred to as the "king of nonsense." Most limericks begin, "There once was a . . . (lady or man) of . . . (some specific place like Nantucket)" and by the time the poem ends, the lady or man has met with some humorous misfortune surely beyond his or her control. Another characteristic of limericks is that lines one, two, and five rhyme, and so do lines three and four. Limericks also put emphasis on stressed syllables within the lines, and the stress as noted (in caps) in the lines which follow adds to the humor of the poem: There WAS a young LAdy of NIger, Who SMILED as she RODE on a TIger . . ."

Three student examples follow.

There once was a little ol' frog,
Who swam and swam in the marshy bog.
He tried to surface and open his eyes
But, boy oh boy was he in for a surprise
He tried to come up from under but his head bumped square into a log.

       Kevin Rischow

There once was a man who looked like a bear,
And one day he did not know what to wear.
Purple or green, which should he choose:
Plain or red polka-dotted shoes?
All in all, to the ol' man it really didn't matter.

       Christin Luckman

There once was a fat kangaroo,
Who lived his whole life in a zoo.
He put a young croc' in his pouch
That bit him and made him yelp, "Ouch!"
Now, wasn't that a dumb thing to do?

   Mike Julian

Now It's Your Turn

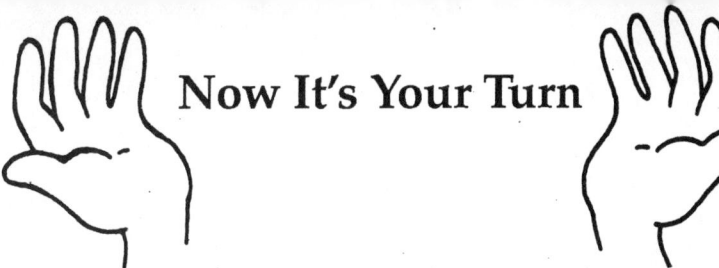

It's time to take your turn at writing poetry. Don't let it scare you. All you need to do is close your eyes and vividly recall an experience you have had–a thunderstorm, birth of a brother or sister, family reunion, or anything that deeply stirred your emotions. For example, have you ever moved? What did it feel like to be told you were going to move? How did you feel when the moving van pulled up in front of your house and the movers began carrying box after box of your family's possessions out to the van? How did it feel to spend the first night in your new home? Who was the first person you met? What did it feel like when you met him or her? Before you begin to write your poem, try to remember a sunset you watched or a picnic your family shared. Keep in mind that your poem needs to be honest, needs to be full of vivid word pictures, and needs to go through the same writing process that all writing needs to go through (brainstorming, draft, "cooking," second draft, editing, final draft, and sharing).

You are ready to begin the fun and serious "business" of writing poetry. Enjoy.

1. Write your own haiku.

_____ (5)

_____ (7)

_____ (5)

_____ (5)

_____ (7)

_____ (5)

Copyright © 1994, Good Apple   GA1491

2. Next, try writing the "formula" five-lined poem called cinquain. Look back at the characteristics of this poem (page 127) before you write two examples on the lines provided for you.

_____

_____

_____

_____

_____

_____

_____

_____

_____

_____

3. Write your own acrostic in the spaces provided. If necessary add boxes and lines to complete your poem. You may even wish to use another piece of paper to bring your poem to its finish.

4. Now write a long free verse poem or two short ones.

A. _____

B. _____

5. Use the beginning three words and write three limericks. Enjoy the humor in this delightful form of poetry. Make the reader, make yourself smile.

There once was
_____
_____
_____
_____
_____

There once was
_____
_____
_____
_____
_____

There once was
_____
_____
_____
_____
_____

Poetry sets you free.

Who Am I? Poems

No one knows you better than you. Writing a poem about who you are can be an interesting, revealing, and challenging task. Traditionally, when you think about who you are, you think about the "face you see in the mirror." But, in fact, you are more than the sum of your physical characteristics. You are a complex creature, unique in all the world. You are one of a kind.

While it is challenging to write a poem about yourself, it is also fun because it lets you let others know who you are. To write a bio-poem, it is a good idea to close your eyes and picture in your mind who you are. Then think of word-images that describe you. Listed below are characteristics which you could use to help you "paint" your portrait. Do not limit yourself to the list. Use it as a springboard of ideas for your poem.

color of eyes, hair
body size, shape
listener
well-groomed
quiet, shy
talkative
understanding
loyal
fair, frank
negative, nervous

clever, funny
stubborn, determined
artistic, athletic
friendly, happy
outgoing
perfectionist
optimistic
dependable
spontaneous
full of life

When writing the poem about yourself, you may choose to write in chronological order (birth to present time), as a metaphor (comparing yourself to an animal or something else), as a narrative (a story), or in other forms already discussed.

Below are some student samples of poems written in response to the question, "Who are you?" Note the varied ways in which they view themselves. You, too, can picture yourself in a variety of ways. Let your imagination guide you. The goal is for your reader to have a clear picture of who you are after reading your poem.

A Thought

"One wish," the genie said.
One wish, I had to think about that.

Harmony on Earth?
Equality?
Ending poverty?

A million things
That I could have chosen
But my heart was selfish and
Begged for just one thing–
My father back.

His towering, lean body
Healthy, cheery, and kind.
With colors pink, yellow, and red.
Until cancer came . . .

This truth brought
Us to the hospital
To cry and make
Tears streak down our faces.
The question, "What is life?"
Was heard more than once.

Then the genie interrupted,
"Will you please make up your mind?
I have things to do
And places to see."

I still wanted to wish for my father's return
But, then, remembered he was at peace.

So my only remark to the genie was,
"I do not want fortune or fame.
I do not want a wish.
Everything's fine."

The genie left without a word,
I sighed and walked away.
At last I understood my dad was at rest.

            Meghann Wu

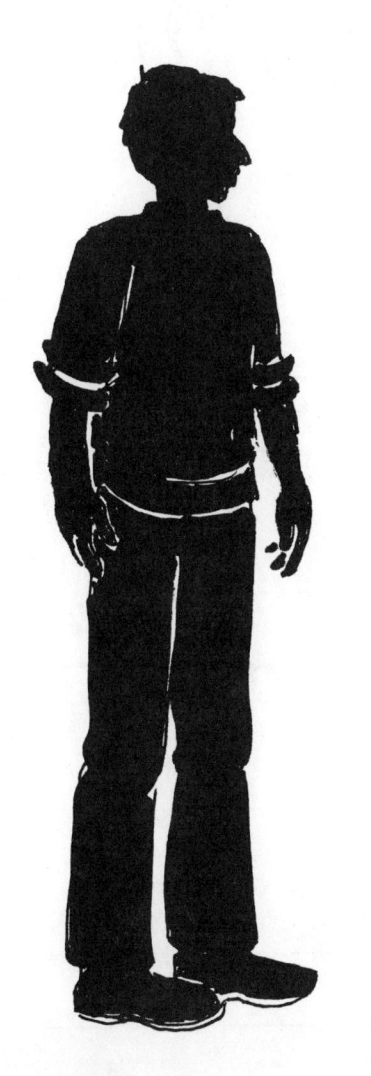

Who Am I?

I am a leader reliable and calm,
trustworthy and arrogant,
and once in a while wrong.

I am lazy and forgetful,
pitiful and kind,
I have some bad memories,
most are left behind.

A friendly kid
with a captivating smile,
a guy who will "go the extra mile."

I am crazy and psychotic,
talented and good,
"I'd do it better than you thought I could."

I always know what to say,
and who to say it to.
Do you really know who I am?
I am really all of you.

                        Parth Amin

The Dolphin

I am a dolphin living under the sea,
I glide through the water swiftly and free.

Avoiding humans with monstrous cages,
this is a battle my species has encountered for ages.
I just want to live my life free as can be,
living right here under the deep-blue sea.

I'm glad God chose me to be one of His creatures,
Enabling me to observe life's fascinating features.
Wish I could live without a care,
wish my troubles were as light as air.

I love my habitat and what it offers me,
and if I were an animal, a dolphin I would surely be.

        R.J. Dorzail

Now It's Your Turn

Who Am I?

Concrete Poetry

Concrete poems are interesting poems in which their themes dictate their forms. For example, if the poem is about a football, the poem will be shaped like a football, and if the poem is about a willow tree, the poem will be shaped like a willow tree. So the poem's shape is determined by what image the poet has in mind when writing the poem. Concrete poems are visually appealing and fun and force you to look at poetry from a different perspective, from a different point of view. While they are fun to construct, concrete poems must be created in the same manner all other poems are created: to offer the reader a fresh, vivid approach to looking at the world in which we live. Concrete poems, like all other poems, must be thought-provoking.

Look at the sample concrete or shape poems which follow on page 142, and try your hand at writing some for yourself. Here's all you need do. First, think of an object, saying, or action which appeals to you. Next, write a poem in the shape of the image you are planning to convey. To get started, you might begin by drawing the shape of the image you have in mind, and then you could superimpose words or letters over the shape to create the physical image you want to impart to your reader. Later, you may want to erase the shape you have drawn, leaving only the words or letters behind, or you may elect to have your final poem represented by both images.

Suggested themes for your concrete poems:

Shapes

- A sports car
- A basketball hoop
- A telephone
- A castle

Sayings

- April showers bring May flowers.
- Dog is man's best friend.
- Mind your P's and Q's.
- All that glitters is not gold.

Actions

- A flowing river
- An erupting volcano
- A speeding car
- An Alpine skier racing down a steep slope

Some sample concrete poems:

SQUARE
SQUARE
SQUARE
SQUARE

PIGSKIN · PIGSKIN · PIGSKIN
PIGSKIN · PIGSKIN · PIGSKIN
PIGSKIN · PIGSKIN
PIGSKIN
PIGSKIN · PIGSKIN · PIGSKIN
PIGSKIN · PIGSKIN · PIGSKIN

Teddy bears are for young and old.
They are to people as silver is to gold.
Teddy bears are warm and cuddly,
make you feel safe in bed,
even if they lose an eye or nose or begin to shed.... There is something about their faces, the twinkle in their eye, and they're always there to hug, or when you need a good, hard cry....
Buttons, Ted whatever the name, I'll still love my teddy bear all the same.

A. Anderson

Now It's Your Turn

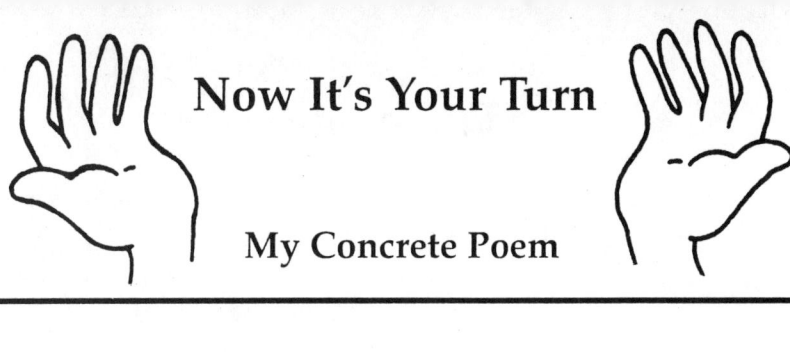

My Concrete Poem

Diamante

A **diamante** (dee-ah-mahn-tay) is a diamond-shaped, seven-lined poem that moves from one idea to its opposite. This is how it works:

Line 1: noun   (subject to begin the poem)
Line 2: adj. adj.   (describing the noun)
Line 3: verb verb verb   (each ending in "ed" or "ing" and relating to the noun in line 1)
Line 4: noun noun noun noun   (2 are related to line 1, 2 suggest change to line 7)
Line 5: verb verb verb   (also ending in "ed" or "ing" but related to line 7)
Line 6: adj. adj.   (describing line 7)
Line 7: noun   (opposite to noun-subject in line 1, ends the poem)

EXAMPLES

Day
Bright, cheerful
Shining, warming, blazing
Daybreak, sun, shadows, sunset
Cooling, darkening, nearing
Mysterious, dark
Night

Anonymous

Enemies
Silent, bitter
Fighting, hating, hurting
At last face to face
Asking, thinking, hoping
Talking, laughing
Friends

Anonymous

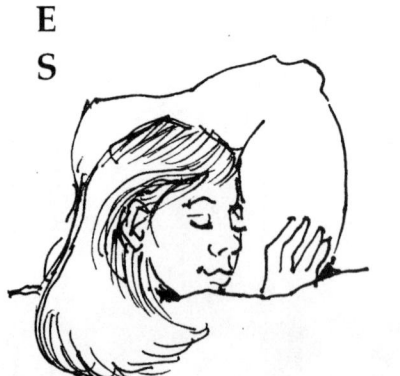

Morning
Crackling, crisp
Glistening, gleaming, glaring
Sun that stings my face
Rushing, raging, tiring
Soothing, sleepy
Evening

Anonymous

Now It's Your Turn

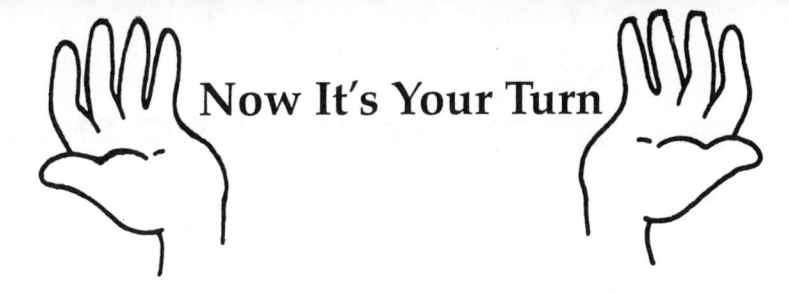

My Diamante

1. Noun _____
2. Adj., Adj. _____
3. Verb, Verb, Verb _____
4. Noun, Noun, Noun, Noun _____
5. Verb, Verb, Verb _____
6. Adj., Adj. _____
7. Noun _____

1. Noun _____
2. Adj., Adj. _____
3. Verb, Verb, Verb _____
4. Noun, Noun, Noun, Noun _____
5. Verb, Verb, Verb _____
6. Adj., Adj. _____
7. Noun _____

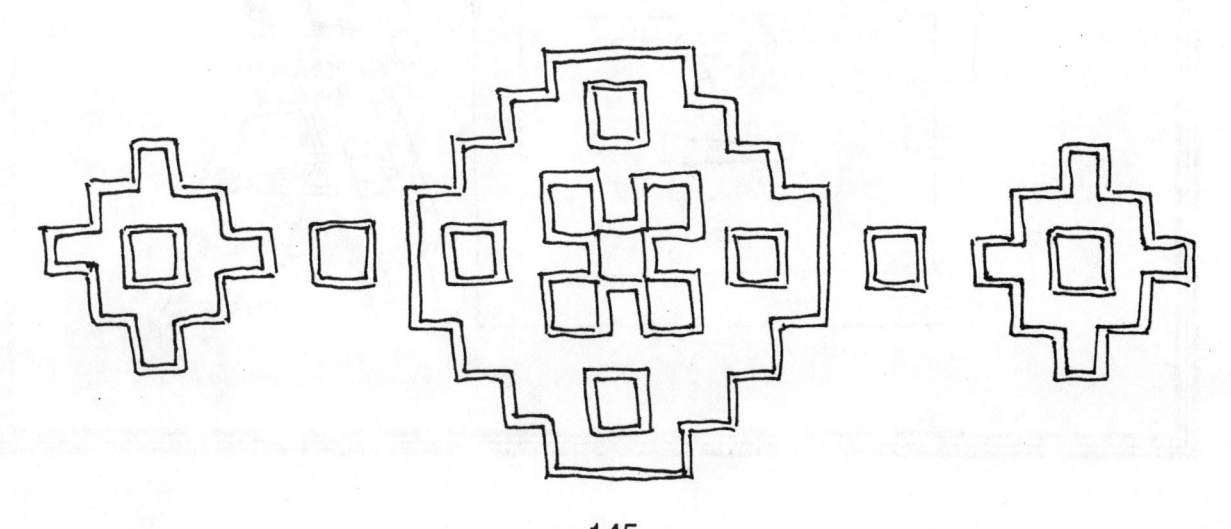

Index

Index

A

acrostics 128-129, 134

addresses (see letters)

  envelope 81-82

  letters 77-82

  for publication 86-89

adjectives 18-21

  predicate 18-20

adverbs 19-21

alike and different 9, 13

alliteration 120, 125

anthology 37

apostrophe 120, 125

assonance 120, 125

B

bandwagon technique 68, 69

banners 98-101

beginnings (for stories) 41, 42, 44

body (of letter) 77-80

book reports 92-97

brainstorming 29, 31, 133

C

caesura 120

cause and effect 8, 12, 68

character (story) 38, 39, 45, 47

cinquain 127, 128, 134

circling and detailing 8, 12

climax (story) 40

collages 102, 103

compare and contrast 26, 27, 64, 65

concrete poems 141-143

conferencing 32, 34

conflict (story) 45, 46

conjunction 21

contests (writing) 89

cover letter 86

D

denotation 121, 125

descriptive writing 50-58

descriptive "lingo" 52-54

diagramming an idea 9, 14

diagramming sentence guide 17-20

diagramming sentences 17-25

diagrams, Venn 26, 27

diamante 144, 145

diaries 72-73, 76

drafts (writing) 31

E

editing 32, 34

ending (story) 40-41, 43, 44

envelopes 81-82

expository writing 59-65

F

fiction 41-43

free verse 129-131, 135

G

grammar (see specific elements)

H

haiku 126-127, 133

hyperbole 122, 125

I

identifying problems and solutions 10, 14

image/imagery 38, 50, 51, 55, 56, 122, 125

interjection 21

introduction (story) 39, 41-42, 44

irony 122, 125

J

journals 72-75

K

KWL (know, want to know, learned) 7, 11

L

lead (story) 41-42

letters

  business 77-79

  cover 86

  friendly 78, 80

  how to fold 83

  query 86

likenesses and differences 9, 13

limerick 132, 136

"loaded" words 68

M

mapping

  diagrams 9, 13

  writing 29

metaphor 122, 125

meter 122

middle (story) 39-40

mobiles 108-113

N

narrative writing 38-49

nonfiction 42-43, 97

nouns 17, 21

O

onomatopoeia 123

opinion (see persuasive writing)

  bandwagon 68-69

  propaganda 68-69

organizers 5-16

outlining 15, 16

P

parts of speech (see specific parts)

personification 123, 125

persuasive writing 66-71

photo essay 37

plot (story 38-39, 45-46)

poetry

  acrostics 128-129, 134

  concrete 141-143

free verse 129-131, 135

limerick 126, 132, 136

Who Am I? 139

posters 37, 104-107

predicate nominative 18

preposition 19-21

prewriting

brainstorming 29, 31, 133

mapping 29, 31, 133

problems and solutions 10, 14

projects 91-117

banners 98-101

book reports 92-97

collages 102-103

mobiles 108-113

posters 104-107

puppet people 114-115

shoe box float 116-117

pronouns 20, 21

proofreading 32, 34, 133

propaganda 68-69

publishers 86-88

publishing 32, 35-37

publishing (getting) 85-90

puppet people 114-115

Q

query letters 86

R

reading, SQ3R 6

rhyme 123, 125

rhythm 124

S

SASE 86

schedule 2-4

sensory images (see images/imagery) 38, 51, 55, 56, 122, 125

sensory words 51, 55, 56

sharing (writing) 32, 35, 36

shoe box float project 116-117

simile 124, 125

SQ3R (see reading) 6

stanza 124

story

characters 38, 39, 45, 47

plot 38, 39, 45, 46

setting 45, 47

title 38, 40

story telling (see narrative writing) 38-49

study skills 2-4

subject "You" understood 18, 23, 24

subject (sentence) 17-18

symbol/symbolism 124-125

T

testimonial words 68

titles (story) 38, 40, 46

U

V

Venn diagrams 26-27

verbs 17-21

  action 17, 21

  state of being 17, 21

verse 124

W

W"s," who, what, where, when, why 6

Who Am I? poems 137-140

writing

  brainstorming 29, 31, 133

  descriptive 50-58

  draft 31, 33

  expository 59-65

  letters 77-80

  mapping 29

  narrative 39, 40

  persuasive 66-71

  process 31-37

  sharing 32, 35-36

  thank-you notes 77-78, 80

writing process

  "cooking" 32, 34

  draft 31, 33

  mapping 29

  proofreading, revising, editing 32

  web 29-30

Y

"You" understood sentences 18, 22-25

Z

Bibliography

Bibliography

Books are listed by main chapters in *Study Starters*.

1. Getting It Together

   Barrington Middle School B.O.S.S. Learning Strategies. 1991.

   Ehrlich, Eugene, and Daniel Murphy. *Writing and Researching Term Papers.* New York: Bantam Books, 1985.

   Ohme, Herman. *Learn How to Learn Study Skills.* Los Altos, CA, Calif. Ed. Plan, 1986.

2. Writing, Writing, Writing

   Atwell, Nancie (ed). *Coming to Know Writing in the Intermediate Grades.* Portsmouth, NH: Heinemann and Cook, 1990.

   Benjamin, Carol Lea. *Writing for Kids.* New York: HarperCollins Publishers, Inc., 1985.

   Bradbury, Ray. *Zen in the Art of Writing.* New York: Bantam Books, 1990.

   Calkins, Lucy McCormich. *The Art of Teaching Writing.* Portsmouth, NH: Heinemann and Cook, 1986.

   Carroll, David L. *A Manual of Writer's Tricks.* New York: Paragon House, 1990.

   Elbow, Peter. *Writing with Power.* New York: Oxford University Press, 1981.

   _____. *Writing Without Teachers.* New York: Oxford University Press, 1973.

   Kirby, David and Tom Liner with Ruth Vinz. *Inside Out 2nd Edition.* Portsmouth, NH: Heinemann and Cook, 1988.

   Maleska, Eugene T. *A Pleasure in Words.* New York: A Fireside Book, 1981.

   Marius, Richard. *A Writer's Companion.* New York: McGraw-Hill, Inc., 1991.

   Mueller, Lavonne, and Jerry D. Reynolds. *Creative Writing.* Lincolnwood, IL: National Textbook Co., 1990.

Naylor, Phyllis Reynolds. *How I Came to Be a Writer.* New York: Aladdin Books, 1987.

Provost, Gary. *100 Ways to Improve Your Writing.* New York: New American Library, 1985.

Roman, Kenneth, and Joel Ralphaelson. *Writing That Works.* New York: Harper & Row, Publishers, 1981.

Writer's Digest Magazine. F. & W. Pub., Inc.; 1507 Dana Ave.; Cincinatti, OH 45207.

Yates, Elizabeth. *Someday You'll Write.* New York: E.P. Dutton and Co., Inc., 1969.

Zinsser, William. *On Writing Well (3rd edition).* New York: HarperCollins Publishers, Inc., 1988.

_____. *Writing to Learn.* New York: HarperCollins Publishers, Inc., 1988.

3. Make, Take, Invigorate

Arnold, Arnold. *The Crowell Book of Arts and Crafts for Children.* New York: Thomas Y. Crowell, 1975.

Marks, Mickey Klas. *Collage.* New York: The Dial Press, 1969.

_____. *The Woman's Day Book of Gifts to Make.* New York: Simon & Schuster, 1976.

4. Poetry Gives Voice to Our Silent Songs

Grossman, Florence. *Getting from Here to There–Writing and Reading Poetry.* Portsmouth, NH: Heinemann and Cook, 1982.

Heard, Georgia. *For the Good of the Earth and Sun (Teaching Poetry).* Portsmouth, NH: Heinemann and Cook, 1989.

Henderson, Harold G. *Haiku in English.* Rutland, VT: Charles E. Tuttle Co., 1985.

Hopkins, Lou Bennett. *Pass the Poetry Please!* New York: HarperCollins Publishers, Inc., 1987.